HADRIAN'S CYCLEWAY

About the Authors

Carl McKeating and Rachel Crolla live on the edge of the Yorkshire Dales. They are outdoor pursuits all-rounders, with specialisms in climbing and mountaineering; Rachel notably became the first woman to reach the highest point of every country in Europe in 2007. The couple had their earliest cycling adventures together as teenagers in 1994. They learnt the hard way by carrying camping gear for nine days on their first extended cycle tour round the north of England in 1996, with the Buttertubs Pass between Wensleydale and Swaledale – famously used on the opening stage of the 2014 Tour de France – proving the toughest challenge (although the following descent with dodgy brakes was also interesting!). Carl attempted to cycle to Egypt during winter the following year – a tour that was cut short at the Somme by his bike's ball-bearings having ground to a paste. In the early 2000s the couple cycled Sustrans' C2C and a six-day version of the Walney to Wear ride that finished on Holy Island. In 2018 Rachel Crolla's guide *Cycling the Way of the Roses* (Cicerone) was published; her work on the book inspired Carl to ride the whole 170-mile tour in a day. The couple have enjoyed fostering a love of cycling in their two children and have included many family cycle routes in their recent book, *Outdoor Adventures with Children: Lake District* (Cicerone, 2019).

Other Cicerone guides by the authors

Cycling the Way of the Roses (by Rachel Crolla)
Europe's High Points
Outdoor Adventures with Children – Lake District
Scrambles in Snowdonia (with Steve Ashton)
Walking in the Auvergne

HADRIAN'S CYCLEWAY

COAST-TO-COAST CYCLING
FROM RAVENGLASS TO SOUTH SHIELDS

by Carl McKeating and Rachel Crolla

JUNIPER HOUSE, MURLEY MOSS,
OXENHOLME ROAD, KENDAL, CUMBRIA LA9 7RL
www.cicerone.co.uk

© Carl McKeating and Rachel Crolla 2020
First edition 2020
ISBN: 978 1 78631 042 2

Printed in Singapore by KHL Printing using responsibly sourced paper.
A catalogue record for this book is available from the British Library.
All photographs are by the authors unless otherwise stated.

Route mapping by Lovell Johns www.lovelljohns.com
© Crown copyright 2020 OS PU100012932.
NASA relief data courtesy of ESRI

Updates to this guide

While every effort is made by our authors to ensure the accuracy of guidebooks as they go to print, changes can occur during the lifetime of an edition. Any updates that we know of for this guide will be on the Cicerone website (www.cicerone.co.uk/1042/updates), so please check before planning your trip. We also advise that you check information about such things as transport, accommodation and shops locally. Even rights of way can be altered over time.

We are always grateful for information about any discrepancies between a guidebook and the facts on the ground, sent by email to updates@cicerone.co.uk or by post to Cicerone, Juniper House, Murley Moss, Oxenholme Road, Kendal, LA9 7RL.

Register your book: To sign up to receive free updates, special offers and GPX files where available, register your book at www.cicerone.co.uk.

All of the research, editorial and design work for this guide was completed early in 2020 before the coronavirus lockdown, and the guide was printed during this period. There may be changes to the route as a result, particularly in relation to accommodation and other facilities. Please bear this in mind and let us know of any changes you encounter. Any updates we receive will be reviewed by the authors and shared on the Cicerone website.

Front cover: Passing Hadrian's Wall at Birdoswald (Day 2)

CONTENTS

Sycamore Gap (Day 2A)

Acknowledgements

Thanks in particular to Louise Robinson for coming along on our first experience of the ride. Likewise thanks to Chris Truss for an early start in order to cycle Day 1 and having to pose for our photos at Sellafield – which intrigued the police security! Thanks to the energetic three sisters – Esther, Kate and Sarah Robinson – who were using part of Hadrian's Cycleway (HCW) on a tour connecting Snowdon, Scafell Pike and Ben Nevis and who recommend beginning HCW with a hike up Scafell Pike! Thanks also to Matt, Lynne and Phil Robinson for imparting local knowledge of the route and their help with the Emperor Hadrian statue in Brampton.

Thanks are due to our daughters, Heather and Rosa, who have accompanied us on numerous HCW outings – some with later than expected finishes – but who at least had plenty of fun sitting on the car roof cheering on HCW cyclists. Also thanks to Stephanie Crolla, whose caravan proved useful in support of work on days 1 and 2 of this guide.

Symbols used on route maps

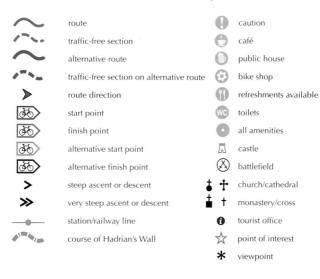

~	route	!	caution
~	traffic-free section	café	café
~	alternative route	public house	public house
~	traffic-free section on alternative route	bike shop	bike shop
>	route direction	refreshments available	refreshments available
start point	start point	WC	toilets
finish point	finish point	all amenities	all amenities
alternative start point	alternative start point	castle	castle
alternative finish point	alternative finish point	battlefield	battlefield
>	steep ascent or descent	church/cathedral	church/cathedral
>>	very steep ascent or descent	monastery/cross	monastery/cross
	station/railway line	tourist office	tourist office
	course of Hadrian's Wall	point of interest	point of interest
		viewpoint	viewpoint

SCALE: 1:100,000

0 kilometres 1 2

0 miles 1

Contour lines are drawn at 50m intervals and labelled at 100m intervals. Route maps are drawn at 1:100,000 (1cm = 1km)

GPX files for all routes can be downloaded free at www.cicerone.co.uk/1042/GPX.

Features on the overview map

	County/Unitary boundary		National Park eg **THE LAKE DISTRICT**
	National boundary		Area of Outstanding Natural Beauty eg *Solway Coast*
	Urban area		

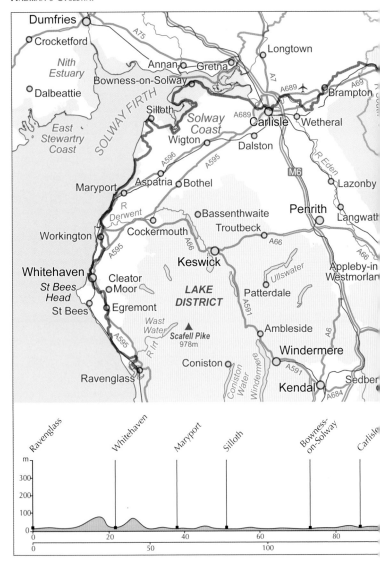

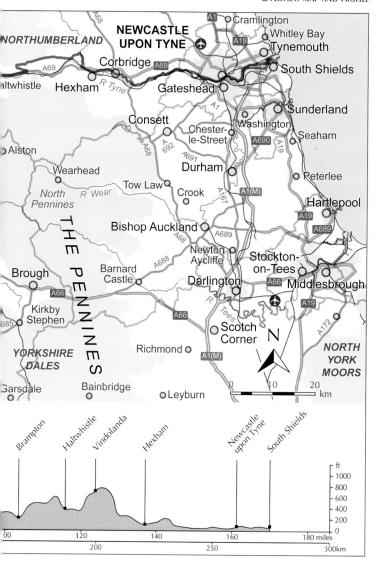

ROUTE SUMMARY TABLES

Hadrian's Cycleway: three-day ride					
	Start	Finish	Distance	Ascent	Page
Day 1	Ravenglass (SD 089 959)	Silloth (NY 110 537)	53 miles (85km)	633m	38
Day 2	Silloth (NY 110 537)	Haltwhistle (NY 705 640)	64 miles (103km)	782m	59
Day 3	Haltwhistle (NY 705 640)	South Shields (NZ 364 680)	57 miles (89km)	953m	90

Hadrian's Cycleway with More Wall Alternative: three-day ride					
	Start	Finish	Distance	Ascent	Page
Day 1	Ravenglass (SD 089 959)	Bowness-on-Solway (NY 223 627)	74 miles (119km)	721m	38
Day 2	Bowness-on-Solway (NY 223 627)	Once Brewed (NY 753 670)	49 miles (79km)	932m	64
Day 3	Once Brewed (NY 753 670)	South Shields (NZ 364 680)	48 miles (77km)	721m	89

Hadrian's Cycleway east to west: three-day ride					
	Start	Finish	Distance	Ascent	Page
Day 1	South Shields (NZ 364 680)	Haltwhistle (NY 705 640)	57 miles (89km)	1050m	118
Day 2	Haltwhistle (NY 705 640)	Silloth (NY 110 537)	64 miles (103km)	680m	83
Day 3	Silloth (NY 110 537)	Ravenglass (SD 088 959)	53 miles (85km)	630m	58

Hadrian's Cycleway the Wall Only: two-day ride					
	Start	Finish	Distance	Ascent	Page
Day 1	Bowness-on-Solway (NY 223 627)	Haltwhistle (NY 705 640)	43 miles (69km)	710m	64
Day 2	Haltwhistle (NY 705 640)	South Shields (NZ 364 680)	57 miles (92km)	953m	90

Hadrian's Cycleway: suggested four-day itinerary				
	Start	Finish	Distance	Page
Day 1	Ravenglass (SD 089 959)	Allonby (NY 081 429)	42 miles (68km)	38
Day 2	Allonby (NY 081 429)	Warwick Bridge (NY 478 570)	53 miles (85km)	56
Day 3	Warwick Bridge (NY 478 570)	Once Brewed (NY 753 670)	30 miles (48km)	74
Day 4	Once Brewed (NY 753 670)	South Shields (NZ 364 680)	48 miles (77km)	89

Hadrian's Cycleway: suggested five-day itinerary				
	Start	Finish	Distance	Page
Day 1	Ravenglass (SD 089 959)	Maryport (NY 081 429)	37 miles (60km)	38
Day 2	Maryport (NY 081 429)	Burgh by Sands (NY 320 590)	45 miles (72km)	54
Day 3	Burgh by Sands (NY 320 590)	Gilsland (NY 632 666)	29 miles (47km)	68
Day 4	Gilsland (NY 632 666)	Corbridge (NY 989 645)	32 miles (52km)	80
Day 5	Corbridge (NY 989 645)	South Shields (NZ 364 680)	31 miles (50km)	102

Hadrian's Cycleway: suggested two-day itinerary				
	Start	Finish	Distance	Page
Day 1	Ravenglass (SD 089 959)	Brampton (NY 529 611)	103 miles (166km)	38
Day 2	Brampton (NY 529 611)	South Shields (NZ 364 680)	71 miles (114km)	77

Milecastle 39 near Sycamore Gap on the More Wall Alternative (Day 2A)

INTRODUCTION

Hadrian's Wall from Birdoswald with Walltown Crags in the distance (Day 2)

Hadrian's Cycleway (HCW) is a magnificent 174-mile (277km) coast-to-coast ride that crosses northern England along the most northerly frontier of the Roman Empire. The route takes in the UNESCO World Heritage Site of Hadrian's Wall and its fascinating settlements, forts, mile-castles, fortlets and turrets. The ride allows cyclists to follow the route of centurions from Glannaventa Fort in Ravenglass to Arbeia Fort in South Shields, connecting many famous vestiges of Roman Britain in between that include Birdoswald, Housesteads, Vindolanda, Chesters and Corbridge Roman Town. Taking time to explore the Wall and its associated forts and settlements will get the most out of the ride. Yet even without the enticing prospect of the Wall, HCW would be tremendous in its own right. Sustrans has done a good job designing the route predominately on minor roads and cycle paths. While a number of towns and cities are connected on HCW, including Whitehaven, Workington, Carlisle, Haltwhistle, Hexham and the extended Newcastle urban area, these are mostly negoti-ated by enjoyable, cleverly worked, traffic-free cycle paths along rivers and dismantled railways. HCW takes in parts of two national parks – the Lake District and Northumberland – in addition to exploring the Solway

Coast Area of Outstanding Natural Beauty. Beginning in Ravenglass, the ride serves up delicate Cumbrian coastal strands overlooked by red sandstone cliffs or skirted by gentle rolling foothills – tamed echoes of the great Lakeland fells. These give way to the wild beauty of the northern Pennines before finally country is exchanged for town and the route snakes along cycle paths beside the River Tyne to the North Sea.

Hadrian's Cycleway, also known as National Route 72, opened in the summer of 2006. It belongs to the Sustrans family of northern coast-to-coast routes that includes the original C2C, the excellent Way of the Roses and the impressive Reivers Route. While there are plentiful Roman points of interest on the official HCW, more could have been made of the most famous sections of Hadrian's Wall; the descent from Greenwhelt Bank to Haltwhistle and the ensuing valley ride on the official route misses the opportunity to see the Wall in its best locations. We have sought to rectify this and, as well as the official route, we describe the More Wall Alternative (MWA) – a variation that enhances the riding experience on the tour and is strongly recommended.

WHY CHOOSE HADRIAN'S CYCLEWAY?

Hadrian's Cycleway makes a perfect short cycle tour. If trying to decide between HCW and other Sustrans coast-to-coast routes, HCW is more road bike-friendly than either the C2C or the Reivers. It also involves considerably less ascent than either of those

Hadrian's Cycleway at Wallsend (Day 3)

The gradient from the trough of Vindolanda delivers the second toughest climb of the route (Day 3)

two routes and quite a bit less than the Way of the Roses further south. It has fewer sections on or near busy roads than the C2C. It is also easier to truncate the route yet maintain the coast-to-coast element: this book includes a description of a Wall Only two-day ride that skips the Cumbrian coast and concentrates on the line of Hadrian's Wall for those cyclists short on time who are looking for a manageable cycle tour that can fit a two-day weekend (see Other itineraries).

HCW particularly lends itself to exploring the many vestiges of the Roman Empire encountered and it is well worth factoring this into your itinerary to really get the best out of the ride. The route also suits making stops in historic towns and villages and replenishing calories in coastal,

upland and riverside tearooms. There is a great choice of accommodation, pubs and restaurants along HCW. Added to the archaeological interest is an array of stunning natural features that colour the route, from impressive coastal beaches and estuaries along the Cumbrian coast to wilder moorland and Pennine scenery – with the Whin Sill on the Northumberland uplands and over which the Wall passes the most impressive.

HOW TOUGH IS IT?

Travelling by bike across the country is a supremely satisfying objective and doing so on HCW is an enjoyable challenge within the reach of almost all cyclists. Of the four main northern coast-to-coast routes, HCW

15

Whinny Hill, the last testing hill on the ride heading west (Day 3)

is unequivocally the least strenuous. That is not to say it is in any way easy, however. While there is significant if somewhat imperceptible height gain on Day 1, the hardest climbing is concentrated on the Pennine sections of Day 2 and Day 3. In respect of this, cyclists wishing to build in extra time for Day 2 and make the most of the Wall might find it advantageous to cover extra distance on Day 1 and finish in Bowness-on-Solway rather than Silloth.

Overall there is no question that, although longer, HCW is considerably easier than the C2C and the wild and adventurous Reivers Route to the north. The Reivers Route is occasionally used as an east-west return by HCW cyclists looking for an extended tour (although it would probably be better to use HCW for the return route if considering a double route itinerary).

Ascent data on cycle routes should always be treated with suspicion as ascent is notoriously hard to calculate; it often tends to be incredibly inaccurate and inconsistent due to variables and shortcomings in GPS apps. In respect of frailties in GPS ascent calculations, we have used the Ordnance Survey mapping tool to provide an at least consistent means by which fair comparisons can be made between four routes.

Based on the OS mapping tool the overall height gain of the four northern coast-to-coast routes with comparisons to HCW are: HCW 2378m; WOR 2829m (+451m/+19%); C2C 3612m (+1234/+52%); and Reivers Route 3365m (+987m/+42%).

Although the middle section of HCW feels lofty, the peak altitude of the route is only 255m. This compares with the C2C at 609m, the Way of the Roses at 402m and the Reivers at 357m. HCW is, however, 37 miles longer than the C2C, although only 4 miles longer than both the Way of the Roses and Reivers Route. While the hardest climb on HCW up Greenwhelt Bank is tough, it is far easier than the hardest climbs on other coast-to-coast Sustrans routes and riders will find the hills on HCW generally more gradual and less sustained.

A fair yardstick is to be able to comfortably ride 50 miles with 700m of ascent and still clamber back onto your saddle the next day. If you can do so, then you will be more than capable of the three-day itinerary. The challenge is naturally increased if planning to carry tents and camping equipment or if prevailing wind conditions work against you.

HOW MANY DAYS?

This book primarily describes the route as a three-day ride within the capability of an average cyclist. For an enjoyable three-day ride, you will need to be saddle fit and have completed some training (day rides of 40+ miles) in the weeks leading up to your trip.

More days will allow extra time to get to and from the route and especially for exploring Hadrian's Wall and the numerous Roman sites

along the way. Regardless of the number of days allocated to the ride, we recommend building time into the itinerary for an unforgettable walk along the Wall from Steel Rigg near Once Brewed (visited on the MWA or accessible by a mile spur from the official route). Four and even five-day tours are not uncommon, allowing more time for sightseeing.

The full HCW in two days would definitely be a very tough challenge and is not really a good choice for average cyclists. It works best with a stop in Brampton. This means 103 miles on what psychologically seems to be largely flat and undulating terrain is covered on the first day and 71 miles including the crossing of the Pennines is covered on the second day. The shortened two-day route, The Wall Only, is a much better option for time-pushed riders (refer to Other itineraries).

The entire HCW has been done as a serious one-day challenge, but the indirect nature of the route combined with other factors means that better one-day challenges can be found.

WEST TO EAST OR EAST TO WEST?

In the main part of this book we describe HCW in a west to east direction. This is the most common direction in which cyclists undertake the ride. This direction takes advantage of the westerlies (winds that blow west to east) that predominate in UK wind patterns. However, westerlies cannot be counted upon and any wind direction on any given day or indeed at any time of a day is possible. HCW is perfectly feasible cycled in an east to west direction. Dutch cyclists who have caught the ferry from Amsterdam to Newcastle seem to account for the majority of cyclists on HCW heading in an E–W direction – invariably using the route as part of a there-and-back coast-to-coast tour.

Conditions to favour an overall E–W crossing in preference to a W–E direction are rare; although prevailing easterlies on the first quarter of the route are not wholly uncommon. If considering an extended there-and-back cycle tour using one of the other Sustrans north England coast-to-coast routes like the Reivers Route, the C2C

or – with an even greater connected loop – the Walney to Wear or Way of the Roses, we feel HCW is the best choice for the E–W crossing. This is partly because of its sheltered nature along the Tyne Valley section and that going N–S between Silloth and Ravenglass is not usually a significant disadvantage when compared to going S–N on that route. E–W might appeal for various other reasons: if you have already completed the ride in the standard direction and wish to see it from a different perspective; if the logistics prove easier that way around; or if your plans are flexible and the forecast is for prevailing easterly winds.

The signage for an E–W crossing is equally as good as it is W–E. Further information for E–W crossings

E–W Dutch tourers near the Roman Army Museum (Day 2)

Looking east across Rapishaw Gap, where the Pennine Way leaves the Wall (Day 2A)

is added at the end of each stage of the route description.

GETTING THERE AND BACK

The first thing to flag up is the end of the ride: an early start on Sundays is advisable to ensure the Shields Passenger Ferry is reached before its **last sailing at 5.45pm** (last sailing Monday–Wednesday 7.45pm; Thursday–Saturday 10.40pm).

By train

For small groups and solo travellers, the train is a viable option. Ravenglass is out on the edge of northern England and is reached by a very slow yet relaxing branch line, the looping Cumbrian Coast Railway. Connections from the West Coast Mainline can be made at either Lancaster or Carlisle.

It is possible to leave your car in Ravenglass and catch trains back from Newcastle using the Tyne Valley Railway and Cumbrian Coast Railway. The fastest time from Newcastle to Ravenglass is 3hr 19min. However, journeys of five hours that involve waiting to change trains are not uncommon. No reservations are needed for bikes and although strictly speaking the trains do not have to carry more than two bicycles at a time if they are busy, this seems to be down to the discretion of the staff. To get from South Shields to Newcastle mainline train station, refer to the end of Day 3: Bicycles on the Metro.

With a support vehicle

This is a fairly popular option, especially for groups. Support vehicles are discouraged from driving large sections of the actual route as this can be inconsiderate to other cyclists.

It is easy to find free and paid parking close to the start and finish of the route. Ravenglass is very small, so please be considerate. The best pick-up point in South Shields is the reasonably priced beachfront car park by the 'Conversation Piece' sculpture at the bottom of the hill below the official end of the ride at Arbeia Roman Fort – although considerate free parking on the residential streets around the fort is also viable.

Hired return transport

A few companies offer return transport between Newcastle and Ravenglass either before you start or after you complete the ride. Some of these can organise a package combining accommodation and transport (see Appendix B).

By bike and longer tours

It is worth considering combining HCW with one of two other classic Sustrans coast-to-coast routes: the fantastically wild and 'I have not seen a car for hours' quiet Reivers Route or the original C2C route. Both of these routes begin and end in Whitehaven and Newcastle's Tynemouth, respectively. If reversed, they leave only 22 miles of flat riding along HCW's outbound route to Ravenglass. If combining with one of these, we recommend HCW for the return leg.

There is ample accommodation along the route, wherever you choose to break up the ride. A detailed list of accommodation is provided in Appendix A. Advanced accommodation booking in spring and summer in the region of the Wall is recommended for this route, even if you're camping. Silloth and Bowness-on-Solway are both excellent places to stop at the end of the first stage. For Day 2, we recommend adopting the MWA and staying overnight close to the Wall in or around Once Brewed to fully take in the atmosphere of the most iconic sections of Hadrian's Wall. It is worth noting that campsites in the vicinity of the Wall tend to be more expensive than might be expected. While it is a logical stop at the end of Day 2 on the official HCW route, Haltwhistle is fairly unremarkable and cyclists may prefer the small village of Bardon Mill a few miles beyond.

A question frequently asked is what kind of bike should I use to do Hadrian's Cycleway? The answer is simply to use a bike that you are comfortable riding and the capabilities of which you know well. For a successful long-distance ride, worry less about the type of bike you have

Hadrian's tourers passing the mighty Hayton Walnut Tree (Day 2)

and more about whether your bike is in good condition. If, like us, there are limits to your mechanical expertise, then it is well worth taking your bike to the local shop for a pre-HCW service. For the cost – which might only be £20 if everything is in order – weigh up the inconvenience of having to do any major running repairs en route or having to quit the ride. Make sure that your bike is set up correctly for you – you will be on it for long consecutive stretches.

Road bikes

The dropped handlebars of road bikes mean that you can vary your riding position and be faster and more aerodynamic on flat and downhill stretches. Many would-be Hadrian's Cycleway riders are worried by the mention of off-road sections on the route and wonder whether they will cope on a road bike. Our opinion is that with care the ride is just feasible on a road bike without the need for any road-only detours. There are, however, two significant sections on the official route that stretch the limits of what the average road bike user will accept: the 1800m of raised sandy path from Seascale to Sellafield and the unsurfaced last 1 mile to Allonby. A 1km section of the MWA is also unsurfaced and only just passible on a road bike. We have included road alternatives for all these sections.

Touring bikes

A touring bike is ideal for the route, especially if carrying luggage. Touring bikes range from more robust, specially-designed road bikes with dropped handlebars to hybrid style bicycles. Touring bikes are adapted to fit with longer cycle routes and comfort in mind rather than necessarily speed. They tend to come with more fixtures on which to place both front and rear pannier racks, can have long wheelbases and may include subtle seat and front fork suspension systems.

Hybrid bikes

Hybrid bikes are also a good choice for HCW and tend to offer wider tyres which although generally less efficient on roads, add comfort and reassurance for off-road cycling on paths and farm tracks.

Tandems

Tandems are another option; although the narrow off-road path from Seascale would be a challenge. Beyond that section, experienced tandemists should be able to stay in the saddle with perhaps one or two exceptions. There are very few narrow traffic stopper posts and gates that have to be negotiated. The willingness of rail operators to accept tandems on trains and the space and provision for them varies. As well as checking with rail operators when planning your journey, the Tandem Club's website gives a good breakdown of what the existing rules and requirements of rail operators are (www.tandem-club.org.uk/files/information/trains/index.html). Oddly enough, National Express coaches will often accommodate tandems and can prove a more straightforward alternative to train carriage for certain routes.

Electric bikes

Electric bikes that assist cyclists on uphill sections by a power boost have

Two's company – tandem on the route beyond Corbridge (Day 3)

seen an increase in popularity everywhere in recent years. They can be a godsend and open a lot of doors especially for cycle tourers whose age, physical wear-and-tear, illness or physical disability might otherwise make long-distance riding prohibitive. They are certainly not an uncommon sight on HCW.

EQUIPMENT

Ensure you do not forget the following:
* bike lights
* spare inner tube or tubes
* tyre levers
* pump
* Allen keys
* puncture repair kit
* bell
* A lightweight bike lock may be useful

For those who rarely do cycle tours, ensure you know how to replace a punctured inner tube before setting off.

Hydration is crucial, so don't forget water bottles. Most riders prefer to carry two bottles of up to 1 litre capacity in frame cages, but the ride never goes too far from places to fill up water if needed.

It is essential to carry some emergency energy food, even if regular café stops are planned. Never underestimate the impact that a few calories can make on your ability to get up that hill! A full-blown sugar crash is not the reserve of Tour de France cyclists and seems to be a greater risk when cycling than say when hiking or running. One of the authors has had a cycling sugar crash (while cycling the Way of the Roses in a single day) and can vouch for the restorative wonders of an emergency chocolate bar!

CARRYING YOUR GEAR

In cycling, travelling light is a top priority. There is a baffling variety of ways to carry gear.

Panniers are a long-standing good choice for cycle tourers. A rack frame is needed in order to use them. (Pannier racks exist that can be fitted to road bikes that do not have rack fittings.) Cyclists wishing to carry oodles of camping equipment might add front panniers. Some people feel that panniers adversely affect the handling of their bike, cause excessive wind resistance and are cumbersome. If using only one pannier, it should be mounted on the side of the bike away from traffic. If you have never ridden loaded before, it is advisable to do a few practice rides fully loaded before you set out on a multi-day tour.

Heavy rucksacks should be avoided: the body's seated position while cycling would incur excessive wear on your shoulders and neck from a heavy rucksack. A small daysack is a viable option if travelling light, however.

Saddle packs with capacities of up to 17 litres are absolutely amazing for those able to travel light and looking to avoid the wind resistance of panniers.

A **saddle bag** for those travelling super light is an option, especially if a support vehicle is meeting you at the end of each day. Three litre, seat-pack saddle bags are widely available and a good choice for those just carrying the absolute minimum and making maximum use of the pockets of their cycling jersey. Triangular frame bags and handlebar bags can also provide extra storage.

WHAT TO WEAR

Helmets

We recommend them – they are obviously beneficial in the event of an accident or collision, but it comes down to personal preference. There is no current UK law forcing cyclists to wear helmets. In their favour, helmets are now lightweight, allow airflow to the head and can hide bald patches!

Clothing

Most people will find that cycling-specific clothing is useful. Cycling shorts or tights are padded in the right areas and improve comfort during long days in the saddle. Cycling jerseys usually have several useful features: high visibility colours, reflective strips, dropped backs to avoid a draughty gap and easily accessible back pockets – it's amazing how much gear and food you can cram into these. A lightweight waterproof is also a must. Cycling-specific models include reflectors, pockets and longer backs and are generally designed to pack away compactly.

Well-equipped with panniers and saddle packs (Day 3)

Scotland across the sea on the Allonby approach (Day 1)

Many people feel cycling gloves give better grip and reduce handlebar vibration. They are a very good idea outside of summer, as is an earband. Cycling glasses are especially useful if you're prone to runny eyes or you wear contact lenses.

Footwear

It is best to choose shoes you have worn in, rather than a brand new pair. Most types of trainer will suffice for HCW (the authors have favoured lightweight approach shoes).

Specific cycling shoes are an option. Theoretically these are made with efficient transference of power in mind – although recent research has suggested they may be less efficient than trainers for average cyclists because they can encourage upward pulling on the pedals. Cycling shoes with a firm plate sole and cleat are an option, but these are less suitable to off-bike activities. Cycling and mountain biking shoes with recessed cleats that act more like a trainer when off the bike are now popular and probably a better option for a cycle tour.

Unless you particularly want to waste storage space by taking extra shoes for the evenings, consider that your choice of footwear will need to cover all eventualities including potential walks along Hadrian's Wall. Many seasoned cycle-tourers swear by the carrying of Crocs, flip-flops or lightweight sandals to change into for evening relaxation.

MAPS AND APPS

The maps in this book, along with the detailed route descriptions, should provide everything you need to do HCW. A Sustrans map of the route is available at the same scale as the maps in this book. For those who wish to have more detailed mapping, the route is covered at 1:25,000 scale by the following OS sheets: 0L6; 303; OL4; 314; 315; OL43 AND 316. The Ordnance Survey now offers access to all its British maps on computers and mobile devices for a small fee. Other apps such as Viewranger allow users to access parts of OS mapping for a small fee and use Opencyclemap to provide larger scale free maps.

Apps such as Strava and those on Garmin and Apple devices have become increasingly popular for logging rides and comparing times. They can be very useful for working out expected average speed and timings. One word of caution: beware of assuming that the distances and particularly cumulative height gains shown on GPS-based maps are exact. We have found on this route and other cycle tours that the route may be the same, but the total ascent data in particular varies wildly.

SIGNAGE

As of 2020, HCW is impressively well signed with the small blue pointer signs of the National Cycle Network showing '72' and/or the white outline of a Roman centurion helmet. Very occasionally, turn signs have been swallowed by foliage – we have flagged easily missed signs and turns in the route description.

An example of the pointer signs marking the way (Day 2)

CYCLING DOS AND DON'TS

A significant portion of HCW is on shared-use, traffic-free paths. Be considerate to other users. Slow down – children and dogs often move in unpredictable ways. Ring your bell or call out to pass – no one particularly likes being overtaken by surprise.

The vast majority of the route is on quiet minor roads. Riding two abreast is legal and more sociable but the Highway Code stipulates that cyclists should return to single file on narrow roads or bends. It is also good practice to move into single file to let cars pass with ease. Make a point of thanking considerate drivers, even those who are merely doing the right thing; it is good karma and it might encourage drivers to continue respecting cyclists.

Scan well ahead for hazards; unmarked bends, road furniture, grit and livestock detritus are all common on this route.

Remember to use hand signals at junctions unless conditions make it unsafe to do so. If in any doubt, the Highway Code is worth consulting (www.gov.uk/guidance/the-highway-code/rules-for-cyclists-59-to-82).

HADRIAN'S WALL

Considering Hadrian's Wall and the Roman occupation of Britain brings to mind the classic Monty Python sketch, 'What have the Romans ever done for us?' Yet while Britain did indeed inherit advanced concepts of democracy, the building of bathhouses, roads, arches, sewage systems and aqueducts, we perhaps should not forget the Romans were brutal in their conquest and divided the island of Britain in a way that has had a lasting legacy. It is often forgotten, but the construction of Hadrian's Wall essentially seeded the notion of England and Scotland. For good or ill, the Roman occupation continues to exert an influence.

The Roman Emperor Claudius began the gradual process of conquering Britain in AD43. He was followed by Julius Caesar in AD54. Not until the arrival of Emperor Hadrian (Publius Aelius Hadrianus) in AD122 was full conquest of Britain viewed as unlikely. Hadrian oversaw the construction of a wall from what are today Bowness-on-Solway to Wallsend – both of which are on HCW. There was no other structure in the Roman Empire to compare with it.

The Wall was 15ft high, bordered by a ditch filled with sharpened spikes backed up by Vallum – a substantial earthwork much of which remains today – and punctuated by fully garrisoned forts. The idea, occasionally fashionable with some historians, that the Wall was intended as a semi-permeable structure that could function as a customs or trading post of sorts seems wholly misplaced. The Wall was an expensive militarised border. Although a degree of cross-cultural influence was inevitable and elements of what we now refer to as 'Celtic' designs can be traced in some Roman carvings and arte-facts, the notion of cross-fertilisation of cultures is very much overstated. The traditional idea that during the Roman occupation a very different perhaps barbarian culture existed immediately north of the Wall that starkly contrasted with the culture south of it seems far more likely.

Hadrian was succeeded by Emperor Antoninus who tried for-lornly to advance the Empire north-wards and oversaw construction of another wall built largely from turf – the Antonine – in AD142. This stretched between the Clyde and the Firth of Forth, but its defence proved unsustainable and Hadrian's Wall was established as the final limit of the Empire. After the Roman governance of Britannia ceased in the 5th century, the Wall fell into disrepair with much of its stone used for the construction of nearby dwellings. The influence of Rome and its systems of governance largely disappeared overnight. Yet the Wall had existed; it had divided the island, its people and its cultures, and the psychological imprint of a north and south Britain remains today in various forms.

WHO WAS HADRIAN?

Roman emperors were usually colourful characters and Publius Aelius Hadrianus was no exception. Orphaned at the age of 10, young

Looking west along the Wall to Crag Lough and Windshield Crags (Day 3)

HADRIAN'S WALL FACTS

- The Wall runs for 73 miles from Bowness-on-Solway to Wallsend
- The whole defensive structure was roughly 150 miles long, including the fortifications from Ravenglass up the Cumbrian coast to Bowness
- Parts of the Wall were once close to 6m high and 3m wide
- Forts were roughly five miles apart along the Wall. Milecastles were unsurprisingly built at mile intervals generally supported by two intermediary fortlets, each one-third of a mile between
- As well as the Wall itself, the line of fortifications included a ditch, a Military Way and the unique earthwork of the Vallum
- Construction started in AD122 and was largely completed within six years
- It was garrisoned for the best part of three centuries
- The Wall ran parallel to the Roman road Stanegate, which was built about 30 years earlier
- It is thought that the Wall was built from east to west by three legions of men
- Different types of stone were used for the Wall, dependent upon local geology
- The boundary began as a turf wall – parts of which can still be seen

Hadrian was taken into the care of Trajan – his father's cousin who was to become Emperor in AD98. As an adult, Hadrian rose through the ranks of the Roman military and held several public posts including that of imperial ghostwriter. On Trajan's death in AD117 Hadrian became emperor almost by default, despite Trajan never officially signing his adoption or succession papers. Some historians smell a whiff of subterfuge in the exact circumstances of Hadrian's rise to power.

Hadrian's personal life was also fascinating. His unhappy marriage to Sabina (Trajan's great-niece) did not provide an heir and at the age of 48 he met his long term male lover Antinous, who is believed to have only been 13 at the time. The pair travelled together, Hadrian reportedly saving his young lover from the jaws of a lion in Libya, until the then 20-year-old Antinous tragically drowned in the River Nile while on an official tour of Egypt in 130. The drowning again has given rise to a raft of conspiracy theories. Hadrian is thought to have never recovered from Antinous' death and the doomed relationship had a far-reaching cultural impact. Hadrian built the Egyptian city of Antinopolis in honour of his beloved and had his lover deified. A cult that worshipped

Antinous as a god then spread across the Roman Empire and remained popular for a further two centuries.

During his 21-year imperial reign, Hadrian was a cultural leader too – he was the first Emperor to sport a beard and his love of architecture led him to build Rome's Pantheon (still the largest unreinforced concrete dome in the world) and his villa at Tivoli. He travelled to almost every province of the Empire and generally had a less warmongering strategy than his predecessors, aiming to consolidate the gains already made by the Empire rather than seek further expansion. This led him to build not only his famous fortifications across the north of Britain, but on the Danube and Rhine borders as well.

SEEING MORE OF THE WALL

Although parts of the Wall can be seen from the saddle, there is no substitute for getting up close and hiking along a section of the Wall away from the road; it is guaranteed to enhance the experience of your cycle tour. The MWA described in Day 2A is strongly recommended to make the most of the Wall.

A good way to allocate more time to the Wall generally on a three-day tour is to extend the first day and stay in Bowness-on-Solway rather than in Silloth. The best place for a hike is at Steel Rigg near Once Brewed. Steel Rigg is on the MWA, but can also be reached from the official route by a 1.2 mile spur and following 68 cycling signs just before Vindolanda.

Passing remains of the Wall and Milecastle 52 above Banks (Day 2)

Beyond the unsurfaced track on the stunning More Wall Alternative (Day 2A)

From Steel Rigg car park (bike rails) an ideal outing is a there-and-back walk eastwards on a glorious undulating section of the Pennine Way/Hadrian's Wall Path to visit Milecastle 39, the famous Sycamore Gap, Peel Crags and Crag Lough. This is probably the most iconic section of the Wall and really superb. The walk is easily followed to the unmistakable Sycamore Gap (it is 2 miles in total, there and back). Those looking for a longer walk along the Wall could continue to Housesteads Roman Fort (6 miles return). Also from Steel Rigg, walking a mile westwards along another great section of the Wall leads to Windshields Crags – the high point of Hadrian's Wall at 345m and a superb location, especially at sunset.

Walltown Crags near the Roman Army Museum (which is on the fort of Carvoran) north of Greenhead are on the MWA and only 500m off the official HCW. There is a large parking area at Walltown Crags and Quarry (bike rails and toilets). A walk eastwards takes you over an impressive section of the Wall above the crags to Milecastle 45 – roughly 2 miles return.

Milecastle 42 at Cawfield Crags (bike rails and toilets) is also visited by the MWA and well worth a short hike.

The Roman Army Museum above Greenhead does an excellent job of introducing visitors to the Wall and bringing it to life for those who are not well-versed in all things Roman. Vindolanda Roman Fort is the most famous of Hadrian's Roman forts. It has an excellent museum and though

31

Vindolanda with Barcombe Moor and the high point of HCW beyond (Day 3)

much of it can be seen from its perimeter there really is no substitute for wandering among the excavated streets of the settlement.

Housesteads is impressive and perhaps the most romantically situated of the large Wall forts and can be accessed from the official route by a spur (see Day 3). Chesters Roman Fort – famed for its riverside bathhouse – is slightly off route on Day 3 but gives an interesting contrast with its riverside setting; it is a particularly calm and pleasant site. Corbridge Roman Town is also en route just before Corbridge proper. The situation, among houses, of the end of the Wall in Wallsend is perhaps more peculiar than impressive. The similarly peculiar setting of Arbeia Roman Fort and its remains are, however, more extensive and interesting. If time is short, Vindolanda is arguably the most impressive fort to visit.

English Heritage
Members of English Heritage gain free entry to a number of paid-for sites visited by the route, including Lanercost Priory, Birdoswald Roman Fort, Housesteads (also free to National Trust members), Corbridge Roman Town and Chesters Roman Fort. Carrying a membership card is useful.

ALTERNATIVE ENDINGS: RUNNING LATE AND TYNEMOUTH

The final phase of HCW involves a memorable short ferry crossing. The **last Tyne Ferry service** between North Shields and South Shields is: **Sunday, 5.45pm**; Monday–Wednesday, 7.45pm; Thursday–Saturday, 10.40pm. Given the early finish of the service on Sundays – the most common day for cyclists to complete HCW – we have included two alternative methods for completing HCW at the end of the Day 3 route description. The first describes how to reach South Shields and Arbeia Roman Fort using the Tyne Pedestrian and Cycle Tunnel. The second suggests a less satisfying finish at the conventional end point of the C2C and Reivers Route on the

north side of the river at Tynemouth. Neither finish changes the overall route distance of 174 miles.

USING THIS GUIDE

The main HCW route is described in detail in three day sections because this is the most popular way of tackling the ride. Each section has a comprehensive route description and detailed maps, as well as smaller scale ones where the route goes through populated areas. Points at which it is important to pay attention to the navigation are highlighted, as well as potentially hazardous road crossings and descents. Also included in each day section is a route profile, showing where the main climbs and descents of the day take place.

For cyclists running late – the Tyne Pedestrian and Cycle Tunnel (Day 3)

Superb cycling in the valley between Banks and the Swartle with Lanercost Priory beyond (Day 2)

For each section you will find a route information box. This details key information you need to know before going on the ride such as mileage, ascent and refreshment stops. Total ascents are approximate and the gradients mentioned refer to the steepest parts of the climbs. The route information is followed by a brief summary of the key features of the day's riding ahead, followed by detailed directions. Details of worthwhile variations are given at the appropriate points within the description of the main route.

GPX tracks

GPX tracks for the routes in this guidebook are available to download free at www.cicerone.co.uk/1042/GPX. GPX files are provided in good faith, but neither the author nor the publisher accept responsibility for their accuracy.

HADRIAN'S CYCLEWAY

Passing Milecastle 42 on the More Wall Alternative (Day 2A)

THE THREE-DAY RIDE

A three-day ride on the official route is conventionally split up as follows: Day 1 – Ravenglass to Silloth, 53 miles; Day 2 – Silloth to Haltwhistle, 64 miles; and Day 3 – Haltwhistle to South Shields, 57 miles. On this itinerary, the first day with its more gradual climbing is theoretically the easiest – although coastal crosswinds occasionally add extra challenge and there is more ascent than might be expected. The first overnight stop in Silloth, an excellent picturesque coastal resort, has a wide range of accommodation including campsites. The harder climbing on Hadrian's Cycleway (HCW) is on Days 2 and 3. For the second overnight stop in the Haltwhistle area, it is worth noting that camping accommodation options are slightly off route and

may add a little mileage and a spur to your route (or a devious shortcut!). For all accommodation at the end of Day 2, including camping, it is important to book ahead because places within the scope of the Wall have a tendency to fill up on weekends during the summer tourist season. There are ample bed and breakfast options for a final night stop in South Shields.

The strongly recommended More Wall Alternative (MWA) ignores Haltwhistle in preference to more time in the area of the Wall; accommodation in or around Once Brewed serves this option well.

The best itinerary, especially if an early start can be made, is probably to have a longer first day that allows more time to explore the

Cyclist cresting the highest point of the ride (Day 3)

Bardon Mill 'locals' at the scarecrow festival (Day 3)

finest parts of Hadrian's Wall on Day 2. This is especially so if considering the MWA. There are a decent number of accommodation options dotted along the route between Silloth and Carlisle, although the pleasant Bowness-on-Solway is the most logical choice. Bowness is the western limit of Hadrian's Wall. It has a pub, two cafés, a small campsite and three bed and breakfasts, with further campsite options beyond the village. An overnight stop in Bowness gives a first day of roughly 75 miles on what feels like flattish terrain, but somewhat imperceptibly generates 700m or so of ascent.

For those looking for a shorter final day, using the MWA transfers some of the ascent and distance from Day 3 to Day 2. Whether on the official HCW or incorporating the MWA, accommodation at the end of Day 2 can be found dotted along the route between Haltwhistle and Hexham

(see Appendix A). Although doing very little to shorten the final day on the official route, the quieter village of Bardon Mill only five miles beyond Haltwhistle is a fine choice. Bardon has one pub – the Bowes Hotel – a campsite just outside the village, a self-catering option and two or three bed and breakfasts. The Sill YHA at Once Brewed is a popular stop for cyclists, as are a number of campsites and remote bed and breakfasts in its vicinity. The MWA passes Once Brewed, while on the official HCW it is 7 miles after Haltwhistle (although just slightly off route). Staying at Once Brewed significantly means that one of the big climbs of Day 3 is overcome on Day 2. The Sill tends to attract international visitors keen to see some of the best parts of Hadrian's Wall. Going by the official route from Silloth and staying in Once Brewed gives a tough 71-mile second day with a substantial hill climb finish, but this is offset by a shorter final day.

DAY 1
Ravenglass to Silloth

Start	Ravenglass – Glannaventa Roman bathhouse, Walls Drive (SD 088 959)
Finish	Silloth (NY 110 537)
Distance	53 miles (85km)
Total ascent	633m
Steepest climb	A day that feels flat but imperceptibly accumulates a surprising amount of height gain. The steepest climb is on Foundry Road just after leaving Parton. Roughly peaking at a tame 1:10 (10%), the climb lasts for a distance of around 200m.
Terrain	Predominantly on surfaced cycle paths (many on former railway lines) and minor roads. Three significant unsurfaced off-road sections: the first 200m after leaving Ravenglass; 1800m of raised sandy path from Seascale towards Sellafield; and the last mile into Allonby. The path from Seascale with its uneven grid mesh is the most challenging of these. Nonetheless, we have deemed all the unsurfaced off-road sections just passable for road bikes if ridden carefully.
OS maps	OL6, OL4, OS Explorer 303 and 314
Refreshments	Seascale, Beckermet (pub), Egremont, Whitehaven, Parton (Pantry bakery), Workington, Flimby (café), Maryport, Allonby, The Gincase farm park tearoom, Silloth
Intermediate distances	Seascale, 7 miles; Egremont, 15 miles; Whitehaven, 23 miles; Workington, 30 miles; Maryport, 37 miles; Silloth, 53 miles
Note	Cyclists intending to make the most of the Wall by following the MWA on Day 2 (Day 2A) might find it advantageous to cover more distance and ride 74 miles on Day 1 to finish in Bowness-on-Solway.

Given that the route passes right next to the Sellafield nuclear facility and that the scenic aspects of the West Cumbrian coast tend to have been overlooked by tourists, you might be forgiven for having low expectations of this portion of the Cycleway. Rest assured, this is a magnificent day's riding. Day 1 gives a contrasting coastal prelude to the passages of the ride along Hadrian's Wall by skirting the Lake District and working a line up the coast. The scenery is superb and the experiences – especially riding past Sellafield – will live long in the memory.

HCW leaves Ravenglass, moving momentarily inland before reaching Seascale – a village that would be in a tremendous setting if not for having the enormous Sellafield nuclear power plant and reprocessing complex as its backdrop. A fascinating unsurfaced raised sliver of land between the complex and the sea follows, giving an experience that cannot feel anything other than bizarre. An incursion inland connects the historic market town of Egremont and the fishing town of Whitehaven – largely by means of cycle paths on disused railways that avoid the prominent barrier of St Bees Head.

Whitehaven Marina is attractive and a good choice for a stop. An excellent raised path nestled between red sandstone cliffs then curves with the strand and railway to reach Parton. Further cycle paths take you to the centre of Workington, which somewhat flashes by en route to the traditional fishing village of Maryport – another good place for a break. From here a superb cycle path within the Solway Coast Area of Outstanding Natural Beauty leads to the remote coastal village of Allonby. Thereafter, minor roads through pasture work gently, if indirectly, to the village of Silloth – a jewel of the Cumbrian Riviera with its Parisian style cobbles and the ample beachfront parks of Silloth Green, one of the longest and largest extended village greens in England.

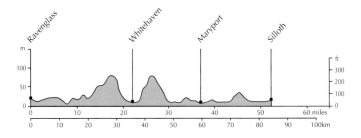

RAVENGLASS

Included within the World Heritage Site 'Frontiers of the Roman Empire', the Glannaventa Roman bathhouse is the only significant surviving structure of Glannaventa Roman Fort. It was likely first garrisoned by Hadrian's forces in the second century and is sometimes regarded as the birthplace of St Patrick – Ireland's patron saint who famously rid the island of its snakes. The bathhouse would have had hot and cold plunge pools and a hypocaust – a type of underfloor central heating system.

The wonderful Eskdale railway built in 1875 makes Ravenglass a popular destination for rail enthusiasts and families in summer. It is affectionately known as 'Ratty' and has a steam train service. Beyond the two railway stations, it seems that Ravenglass has not so much been left behind, as left alone; Georgian terraces overlook small fishing boats and sailing vessels that are tethered by rusty chains to buried stays on mud flats and sand banks. The boats rest on the flats at low tide or loll on muted waves at high tide giving a watercolour quality; little surprise this is the only coastal village incorporated into the Lake District National Park.

The bathhouse at Glannaventa Fort

Looking across the estuary to Ravenglass

If arriving by train, on the exit from the station you will find the customer car park for the Ratty Arms. If arriving by car, there is a paid car park with free public toilets behind the Ratty Arms reached by following the road round from the seafront.

From the Ratty Arms car park turn right and head uphill away from the sea, pass under a bridge of the Eskdale Steam Railway and after a further 100m turn right on Walls Road (signed 72). After 500m, you'll reach the **Glannaventa Fort Roman bathhouse** (also known as Walls Castle). The remains are the official start and they make for a secluded and appealing beginning to both the ride and its Roman theme; there is a small plaque with the information boards to commemorate the start of the route.

With the Roman theme set in motion, the 174-mile tour can truly begin. Retrace the track and turn left on the road towards the sea, passing the train stations. As the road meets the coast and bends sharply left, take a right turn onto a path that leads to a narrow pedestrian crossing attached to a bridge of the Cumbrian Coast Railway. Cyclists are obliged to dismount.

41

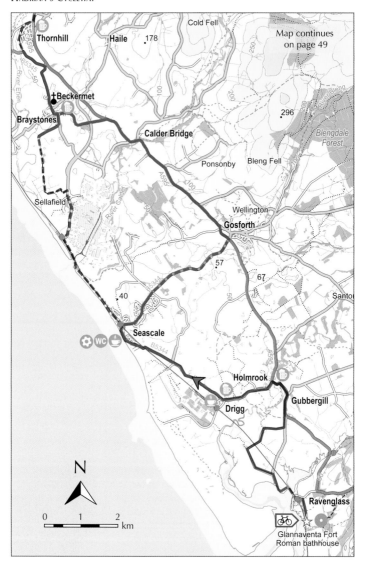

Map continues
on page 49

Follow an unsurfaced track for 400m. ▶ The track meets a road at a collection of houses; after 300m turn left. Just before the next farm, Hall Carleton, take a right turn (as of 2020, the 72 sign here is overgrown).

This track can be subject to flooding during high spring tides, but it is rarely impassable.

On clear days, a distinctive triangular mountain slightly separated from the other Lakeland fells is discernible – this is **Great Gable** at the head of Wast Water. The Scafell massif, which makes up England's highest ground, can be seen to the right.

Pass under a railway bridge and at the T-junction turn left to reach the A595 road. (The bridleway on the left 30m before the A road was once suggested by Sustrans as an alternative route – it is not a viable option.) Turn left on the less than ideal A595 and follow it for 800m to **Holmrook** or consider adopting the little-used pavement set back on the left side of the road; it is not officially designated 'shared use'.

Cross the bridge over the River Irt – its waters are fed by England's highest fells – and take the first left to thankfully escape the A595. A little climb is needed to leave Holmrook and more open pasture briefly intercedes before you pass through the upper part of **Drigg**. ▶ Continue straight on along the B road towards **Seascale**. Just before the village, the sea comes into view and the coast is soon regained.

Just off route, Drigg has a pub and café near its train station.

For a name that has become synonymous with an enormous nuclear facility, **Seascale** is not what you might expect. Its beaches are stunning and the village would be brilliantly situated without the nearby complex – it is little surprise that after the introduction of the Furness Railway in the 1850s, Seascale became a popular Victorian holiday resort. On the hill down to the village, Nebb House is passed. An intriguing ship's figurehead salvaged from a wreck that reputably represents Lord Byron has adorned this former ale house since the Victorian era: 'She cycles in the beauty like the night' perhaps?

Wheel effortlessly down the hill, passing an easily missed ice cream parlour and café on the right before reaching the village seafront, where there is a shop, a butcher, another café and public toilets in the car park. Do not pass under the railway, but instead turn left up a ramp to join the raised sandy path that sits atop an embankment between the beach and railway line. The terrain here is challenging with occasional sand drifts and protruding green plastic grid mesh plates to watch out for.

The path deteriorates where it meets the River Calder and for a brief moment you can be forgiven for thinking a bridge has been washed away. It hasn't. Dismount and follow the disjointed path rightwards under the railway bridge then turn immediately right to discover a hidden footbridge attached to the rail crossing.

Once you've crossed the Calder, continue along a tarmac road. The cycling is now beside Europe's most complex nuclear facility, **Sellafield**, with its high security fences and surveillance cameras; it is a peculiar experience. **While photography is not prohibited, it is worth noting that one of the authors taking photos for this guide was questioned by the police**. Please be tolerant of police interest here; it is, after all, reassuring to know the site is well-secured.

SELLAFIELD

Sellafield, named after the village on which it was built, had an original reactor site called Windscale. Its primary role was to provide plutonium for Britain's first nuclear bombs in 1952. Subsequent adjacent reactors were built to function as the world's first industrial-scale commercial nuclear power plant. The plant, initially called Calder Hall, was opened by the Queen in 1956. In 1957 the world's first nuclear accident occurred when the primary Windscale reactor caught fire. It burned for three days. Although the 'gamble' of turning off the reactor cooling fans and flooding the reactor worked, an ecological disaster on the scale of Chernobyl was only prevented by a very fortunate chimney filter. Physicist Terrence Price, a relative underling, raised concerns about the consequence of a potential fire that most had thought impossible. Against opposition, chief physicist and Nobel Prize winner, Sir John Cockcroft, insisted on a filter being added to the top of the chimney. The filter was added as a complete afterthought. Without the filter – initially dubbed 'Cockcroft's Folly' – the north of England would have suffered long-lasting cataclysmic effects from nuclear fallout.

Soon you'll reach Sellafield train station. From here the route moves away from the coast. Head up the slight hill from the station, following a shared-use cycle path beside Sellafield's perimeter fence. ▶ The shared use path curves rightwards away from the main exit road. After 80m, cross a facility entrance drive, pass under the main

If you still glow in the dark after taking off your high visibility cycling gear, you have been cycling too close!

Steady as you glow: Sellafield nuclear facility with 'Cockcroft's folly' right

access road and continue on an independent cycle path. This path skirts the edges of pasture fields and has a couple of sharp perpendicular turns before joining a dismantled railway. After 1km on the former railway line, the route branches left joining a track and minor road which you should follow to the village of **Beckermet**. Take the left at the T-junction and then another left when you meet the main village thoroughfare. Continue on this, passing the White Mare pub and the distinctive red sandstone of St John's Church, until eventually you reach a junction on a sharp bend of the B5345. Turn left on this and continue until it can be exchanged for a cycle path coming off on the right after 600m.

On-road alternative

A less than ideal on-road alternative is possible from **Seascale** by heading under the railway bridge and staying on the B5344 towards **Gosforth** (make use of a segregated cycle path on the left as Seascale is exited). Leave the cycle path and turn left on the A595. The A595 is the only on-road alternative to the standard route, and although by no means the worst road to cycle along, it is a poor option. Pass through **Calder Bridge** on the A595, then after a mile take a signed left turn to **Beckermet** and rejoin the official route at the White Mare pub.

Where the cycle path meets a housing estate and Woden Road in **Thornhill**, turn left. Follow the road as it bends sharply to the right and blends into Ehen road. Turn left on Thorny Road and uphill to access a cycle path. Turn left on this unattractive part of the route running parallel to a busy stretch of the A595. A short slip road avoids the roundabout and a left leads down to the River Ehen in **Egremont**. A brief climb will take you to the high street. You'll see the ruins of the Norman 12th-century Egremont Castle as you approach the bridge. ◄

Head along Egremont Main Street then turn right onto Chapel Street opposite the library which has a clock tower. Take the first left and follow it rightwards round the warehouses to locate a gated cycle path that

The castle is easily accessed, free to enter and has lots of benches for a stop.

EGREMONT

Egremont annually hosts the Crab Fair – named after the crab apples that were often given away there. This autumn fair has its origins in the 13th century and traditional competitions have involved gurning (Egremont also hosts the World Gurning Championships) and climbing a greasy pole for either a top hat or a side of mutton. Like so many bizarre British traditions, the pole climbing ritual has sadly succumbed to excessive insurance costs. A greasy pole can be seen by the war memorial; it now has spikes to stop any chancers. Wordsworth's poem, *The Force of Prayer* (aka *The Boy of Egremond*) is based on the true story of a potential future king of Scotland from Egremont who drowned while jumping the 'fearful chasm' of the Strid on the River Wharfe in Yorkshire. The jump is not a good idea: like the boy of Egremont, one of this book's authors leapt the Strid in the mid-1990s only narrowly avoiding 'the arms of the Wharfe' and being 'strangled by its merciless force' – as Wordsworth describes.

West Lakeland fells from the cycle path north of Egremont

leads through a tunnel under the A595. Turn left at the road junction, then right at the petrol station along East Road. After 200m, take a left turn off this onto a fairly bumpy shared-use path between a field and a bungalow. Turn sharp right after 150m. The wooded path eventually crosses a bridge over the A5086 to reach a minor road at a lime kiln belonging to the Clints Quarry Nature Reserve; turn right. At the village of **Woodend**, turn right and 80m later turn left off the bend. After roughly 600m, take an easily missed right turn in some trees onto a cycle path that then bears leftwards through fields along a former railway line – if you miss this it is possible to access the cycle path to Whitehaven by heading straight on to meet a bridge in Woodend.

The cycle path soon converges with another former rail line and the route is shared with the C2C. Bear left towards Whitehaven. ◄ Fork left at a triangular green then 100m later turn sharply left to duck beneath a railway line and emerge on a housing estate. Turn right along the residential Wasdale Close, at the end of which a path on the left leads to Crossdale Avenue. Turn right on this to resume the cycle path at the end. This leads

Blue metal posts with decorative railway mining trucks that commemorate the area's industrial heritage complement more orthodox signage.

HCW shares its course with the C2C on the way into Whitehaven

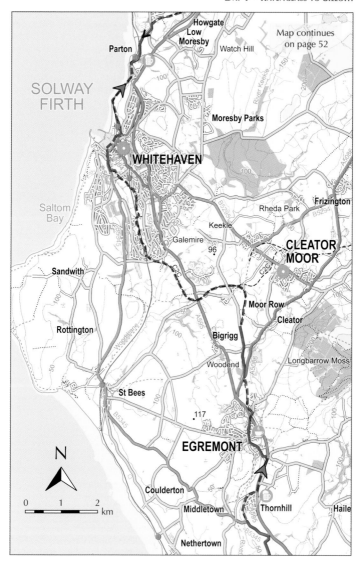

Map continues
on page 52

49

down the right-hand side of a rugby club and under the railway to an immediate left turn. When the path meets a minor road go up a micro hill then turn left along Esk Avenue. After 150m look out for an easily missed left turn onto a cycle path with hairpin bends that ducks under the railway line. ◀ Continue down the side of the football stadium to a T-junction where a right and immediate left lead you back onto a cycle path. You'll emerge on the busy Parson Street. Turn right and after 400m use Quay Street to access the waterfront marina.

The tunnel is not as low at it first appears – but it might be prudent for giants to duck!

At **Whitehaven** marina, turn right on a wide traffic-free area where there is often an ice cream van. From Whitehaven to just outside of Workington, HCW shares its course with another excellent Sustrans ride, the Reivers Route.

At **Whitehaven** marina the eagle-eyed will spot the metal sculpture that marks the beginning of the C2C down a boating ramp. Whitehaven has a rich sea-faring history, which is recognised by its maritime museum and an annual festival. In 1778 the town was attacked by the proto US Navy commanded by John Paul Jones during the American War of Independence. The erstwhile importance of mining in the region explains many of the cycle paths that occupy former mining railways. A distinctive candlestick chimney to the south of the harbour vents a mineshaft of the former Wellington Pit, scene of Cumbria's worst mining disaster in 1910 when 132 miners lost their lives.

A German U-boat fired on Parton, Harrington and Whitehaven in August 1915.

Continue along the pedestrianised marina front until this ends at a seaweed sculpture, where a right turn can be followed by a left briefly onto the A road. Turn left after the petrol station, followed by an immediate left fork to reach a cycle path that arcs majestically round Tanyard Bay poised above the railway and below sandstone cliffs. At the T-junction, turn left to reach **Parton**. ◀

After Parton, the road crosses Lowca Beck and offers up the stiffest climb of the day. Halfway up, turn left on

a busier road and in 100m turn right onto Stamford Hill Avenue. An immediate left is meant to be taken onto a cycle path leading across a playing field: the metal barriers are really awkward, especially if you're heavily loaded. The barriers and playing field path can be avoided by continuing along Stamford Hill Avenue, which soon becomes unsurfaced and curves uphill to meet a lane just to the right of the playing field's exit. Turn right and after 40m adopt the cycle path rather than concrete farm path.

Follow the cycle path for 6 miles to Workington. Take a sharp right turn with an S-bend as you come to an industrial complex. The path then leads you through Workington Fire Station, avoiding a large roundabout and adopting a shared-use path on the right of Moorclose Road. Branch off Moorclose Road after 200m or so onto a secluded wooded cycle path that negotiates most of Workington's urban expanse until you reach Central Way at a series of car parks. Head up to the surprisingly easily missed pedestrianised centre of **Workington**.

The proud town of **Workington** is the home of Uppies and Downies, an idiosyncratic sport played only in Workington: the Uppies are participants traditionally

Poised above the railway and below sandstone cliffs of Tanyard Bay

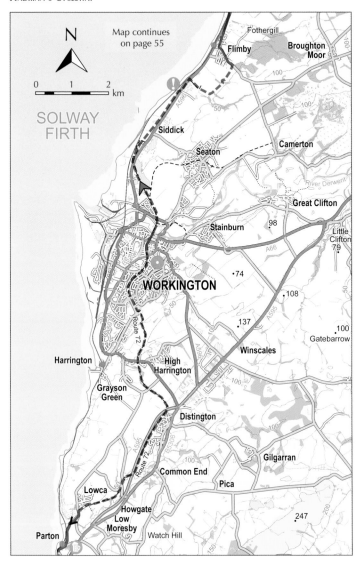

N

Map continues
on page 55

0   1   2
km

SOLWAY
FIRTH

Fothergill

Flimby

Broughton
Moor

Siddick

A595

Seaton

Camerton

River Derwent

Great Clifton

Stainburn

•98

Little
Clifton
•79

A66

•74

WORKINGTON

•108

Route 72

•137

A595

•100
Gatebarrow

Harrington

High
Harrington

Winscales

Grayson
Green

Distington

A595

B5306

Gilgarran

Route 72

Common End

Pica

Lowca

Howgate

•247

Parton

Low
Moresby

Watch Hill

resident in the slightly more affluent upper area of
Workington while the Downies are those whom –
historically at least – would have been resident in the
reclaimed marshes, dockland and coastal dwellings.
Matches have been recorded as far back as the 16th
century and are still played annually. They involve
upwards of 1000 players trying to move a ball – usually by means of a scrum – to the opposition's 'goal'
across town; this often takes hours.

Continue straight on down the hill to pass through
a very dark underpass. Just after this, take the cycle path
forking right and cross over the River Derwent on the
Navvies cycle bridge.

In 400m after crossing the bridge over the main road,
ensure you take the easily missed left turn on the 72. The
cycle path continues, eventually running parallel to the
busy A595. This is eventually crossed and the path continues on the righthand side. At the hamlet of St Helens, turn
right uphill on a circuitous detour. A left onto a gated cycle
path followed by a left downhill leads to **Flimby**. On leaving the village it is necessary to turn right along the A595
for 200m before escaping left onto a pleasant cycle path.

When the cycle path ceases, turn right and follow the
road up to a T-junction where a left leads to the centre of
Maryport. ▶

Workington's Navvies Bridge replaced a bridge washed away by the 2009 floods

Maryport's octagonal lighthouse is one of the oldest cast iron lighthouses in the world.

View towards Maryport's octagonal lighthouse

MARYPORT

The Roman name for Maryport was *Alauna*. It was the site of an important fort, built at the same time as Hadrian's Wall. The remains of the Cumbrian coastal frontier fort can be seen on the hilltop beside the Senhouse Roman Museum, which explains the area's significance to the Romans and show-cases artefacts found locally – the most bemusing of which is an altar stone that Melvyn Bragg described as 'a spectacularly engorged member'. It has a serpent winding round it. Roman Milefortlet 21 is signposted from the route 5km north of Maryport. Its earthworks can be viewed with a five minute climb up the hill beside the coastal path. It is perhaps more impressive than the remains of Maryport's main fort.

Maryport has a rich seafaring history and its maritime museum in the harbour is well worth visiting. Maryport was the birthplace of Fletcher Christian, who famously mutinied on *HMS Bounty*. It was also the child-hood home of Thomas Henry Ismay, who founded the White Star Line that built the *Titanic*. Thomas' son, Joseph Bruce Ismay, was a passenger on the ship's ill-fated maiden voyage in 1912. His subsequent survival was clouded by disputed rumours of him leaving on the first lifeboat at the expense of women and children. The town continues to be a working fishing port. Maryport features in several paintings by 'matchstick man' LS Lowry.

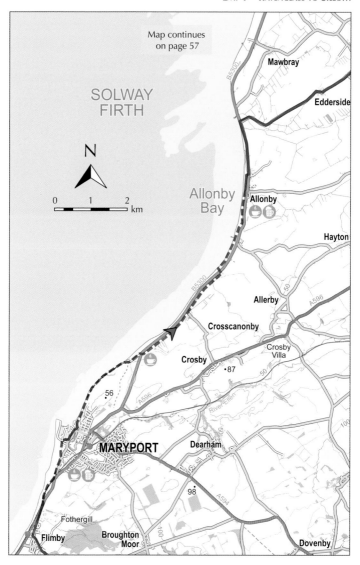

Map continues
on page 57

Mawbray

Edderside

SOLWAY
FIRTH

N

0   1   2 km

Allonby
Bay

Allonby

Hayton

Allerby

Crosscanonby

Crosby
Villa

Crosby

•87

56

River Ellen

MARYPORT

Dearham

98

Fothergill

Flimby

Broughton
Moor

Dovenby

Beyond Maryport: three sisters using part of HCW to connect Snowdon, Scafell Pike and Ben Nevis

The Elizabethan Crosscanonby salt pans are passed between Maryport and Allonby.

Strong Westerlies from the Irish Sea are not uncommon around Allonby

Turn right over the bridge in the centre of Maryport harbour, then immediately left. The road ends at a car park. Continue on a superb traffic-free section beside the sea. This leads to Maryport Golf Club; follow its drive to meet the B5300. Cross straight over this to adopt a cycle path separated from the road by a bank of gorse bushes. After two miles, this crosses back over the road. ◀ The last 1km into Allonby is unsurfaced and can be a little challenging for road bikes, although the easily accessed B5300 is not the worst alternative. The cycle path stops in **Allonby**, a little past some of its shops and cafes.

In 1857 Charles Dickens stayed in **Allonby** with Wilkie 'The Woman in White' Collins at the Ship Inn. He described Allonby as a 'dreary little place'. This is not altogether misplaced: on grey rain-swept days, when westerlies lift spray from the Irish Sea and blast stoic grey rendered buildings on the sea-front, Allonby can take on an austere look. And yet, with its expansive greens and impressive beach, Allonby in its very remoteness proves both a bleak and hauntingly beautiful place where the voices of ancient Cumberland fishermen and smugglers seem to whisper on the wind.

From Allonby, head north for one mile on the B5300 – this can be busy at certain times of the day.

Turn right towards Tarns. After 3 miles of quiet well-signed farm roads, you'll come to a T-junction at **Tarns Dub**. Turn left but after only 100m turn left again. Pass the caravan site beside the tarn. At the next junction, turn left followed by a right in quick succession. Climb over the gentle hill. ▶ Turn right at the next junction, where the popular Gincase Tearoom is situated. After half a mile, there is little warning for a sharp right turn at a farm – this is

The mountains of Dumfries and Galloway are nicely framed across the sea.

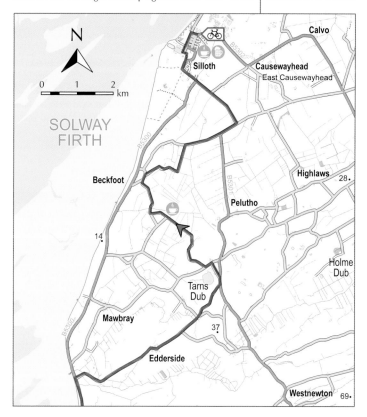

Late season cycling on rain-washed Criffel Street, Silloth

dangerous if taken too quickly because of mud and loose material. The road eventually becomes so little used that grass grows upon its middle tarmac. At the next junction, turn right. Turn left (essentially straight on) for one mile to **Silloth**. At the next junction, turn right. As the road bends sharply to the right, take a left straight ahead onto Links Close, at the end of which is a cycle path that cuts across to Station Road. A left is followed by a right leading to the cobbles of Criffel Street beside Silloth Green.

SILLOTH

Silloth, which reputedly has the largest village green or rather series of village greens in England, was a popular seaside resort in the late Victorian and Edwardian eras. Its tourism was, however, badly affected by Beeching's ruthless branch line closures of the 1960s. There is a hint in the cobbles of Criffel Street and even in its architecture of something continental about Silloth. Although today Silloth is little known beyond Cumbria, the wry moniker 'jewel in the crown of the Cumbrian Riviera' is not altogether unfitting and the village proves a pleasing location to conclude the first day of HCW.

EAST TO WEST

The stage is straightforward E–W. Although the day has more ascent than might be anticipated, there are no particularly difficult climbs, with the steepest of the day being that from the Seascale beach which passes the Byron figurehead.

DAY 2
Silloth to Haltwhistle

Start	Silloth (NY 110 537)
Finish	Haltwhistle (NY 705 640). The quiet Bardon Mill, five miles further along the route, is also a good choice
Distance	64 miles (103km)
Total ascent	782m
Steepest climb	Greenwhelt Bank just after Greenhead is a feisty Pennines beast on a segregated tarmac cycle path that peaks at 1 in 4 – it is the hardest climb on HCW.
Terrain	Predominantly on minor roads with occasional brief interludes on mainly surfaced cycle paths.
OS maps	314, 315, OL43
Refreshments	Kirkbride (Bush Inn with 'cycle pit-stop'); Bowness-on-Solway (Kings Arms and cafés); Burgh by Sands (Greyhound Inn); Carlisle, Assembly Restaurant (an upmarket option, Rickerby); Crosby (pub); Warwick Bridge (pub); Newby Grange Golf Club (café – very pleasant); Hayton (Stone Inn, friendly, weekdays 12–2pm, all day Sat–Sun); Brampton; Lanercost Priory (café); Birdoswald Roman Fort (café); Gilsland (pub); Greenhead (Greenhead Tea Room – super).
Intermediate distances	Angerton-Kirkbride, 12 miles; Bowness-on-Solway, 22 miles; Carlisle, 35 miles; Brampton, 50 miles; Gilsland, 59 miles; Haltwhistle, 64 miles
Note	Cyclists intending to make the most of the Wall should leave the official HCW after the climb from Greenhead and use the MWA (Day 2A) to finish in the Once Brewed area.

This is a great day's riding that exchanges the Cumbrian coast for the soaring tops and intervening valleys of the Pennines, reaching its climax with the appearance of Hadrian's Wall. The ride works round the fascinating Cardurnock promontory with its relics of World War 2 and the Cold War to reach the true beginning of Hadrian's Wall at Bowness-on-Solway. Here, clumps of marsh grass and gorse line expansive estuary sands and mud beyond which Scotland rests in the distance. The firth opens out to unfurl a series of watercolour views and cyclists will relish what is a real highlight of the ride as they zip along a raised road bordering the Burgh Marshes. Carlisle is of course a big urban barrier, but the ride as we describe it sneaks cleverly through the city predominantly on enjoyable parkland and riverside cycle paths. Beyond Carlisle, pleasant if relatively unremarkable country makes for easy riding to the small historic market town of Brampton.

From Brampton the ride climbs into hills and takes on the character for which Hadrian's Wall is famous – snaking a line along stretches of high wild Pennine scenery. A descent to the picturesque Lanercost Priory awaits, before a testing hill climb up to and through the village of Banks with a reward in the surprise appearance of the Wall. The Wall then borders the high line of the route for three miles to Birdoswald. It is on this stretch in particular that you will be able to envision those ancient times when centurions guarded forts and fortlets and barbarians smarted across the moors.

The lofty height of Birdoswald Roman Fort is then exchanged for an interlude of satisfying valley riding that takes in the 12th-century Thirlwall Castle before the village of Greenhead announces that the toughest climb of the ride is imminent – Greenwhelt Bank. Once this is overcome, it is best to follow the stunning MWA. If sticking to the official HCW 72 route, all that is left from the high tops above Greenwhelt Bank is a gradual descent to the small town of Haltwhistle – a claimed geographical 'centre of Britain'. The excellent MWA ignores the descent to Haltwhistle (see the end of this stage).

From the southern end of Silloth Green, follow the cobbles of Criffel Street northwards for roughly 150m. Turn right onto Peteril Street. This soon merges into Wigton Road, which can be a little busy at rush hour. Continue for roughly one mile out of Silloth to reach the hamlet of **Causewayhead**. Take the second of two rights off an initial sharp bend onto quieter roads signed to Blackdyke.

Continue straight ahead through flat farming country to reach a T-junction where you should turn left. After ¾ mile, you'll reach a crossroads with the B5302. Head straight across this to adopt a slightly circuitous, although more pleasant, back route to Abbeytown. At the next T-junction, turn right then continue straight on until you meet the B5307 in the centre of **Abbeytown**.

Barn owl catching a mouse at twilight near Abbeytown

Abbeytown gets its name from Holmcultram Abbey, a Cistercian abbey founded in 1150. Although the abbey was ransacked during the dissolution, its nave now forms part of St Mary's Church and is seen en route at the eastern end of the village. The church suffered an arson attack in 2006 that destroyed its roof, but it has since been restored.

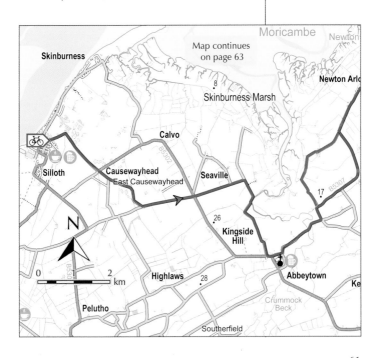

The remains of Holmcultram Abbey are incorporated into St Mary's Church

Turn left along the village main street, but at the first bend take a left (essentially straight ahead) onto the B5307 road (the Wheatsheaf pub on the left is the first building you will pass). It is simplest to follow the B5307 out of the village to pass through **Newton Arlosh** to Kirkbride – which is all signed as the 72. Alternatively, the route originally turned left 1 mile after Abbeytown to pass through Salt Coates – occasionally subject to tidal flooding – before rejoining the B5307 before Newton Arlosh.

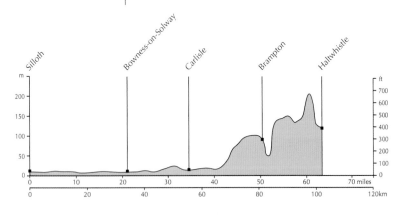

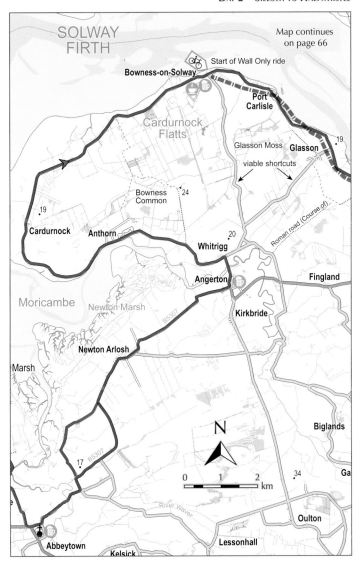

SOLWAY
FIRTH

Map continues
on page 66

Start of Wall Only ride

Bowness-on-Solway

Port
Carlisle

Cardurnock
Flatts

Glasson Moss   Glasson

viable shortcuts

19

Bowness
Common   • 24

19

Roman road (Course of)

Cardurnock   Anthorn

• 20

Whitrigg

Angerton

Fingland

Moricambe   Newton Marsh

B5307

Kirkbride

Marsh   Newton Arlosh

Biglands

B5307

N

17

0   1   2
km

• 34   Ga

Abbeytown   Kelsick   Lessonhall   Oulton

River Waver

The Bush Inn bills itself as a cycling 'pit stop' – it is a good choice for refreshment and has a secure bike lock up.

At a T-junction, you'll spot the Bush Inn at **Kirkbride** just off route. ◄ Turn left. Shortly after a weak bridge over a marshy river a T-junction is reached in **Whitrigg**.

Riders with devious leg-saving instincts or suffering in particularly bad weather will see on the map two considerable shortcut roads that cut out the peninsula, but also the true start of the Wall. Those wanting to look themselves in the eye after finishing the route will turn left and follow HCW as it loops around the Cardurnock peninsula. A strong headwind is not uncommon here. Continue through **Anthorn**, most buildings of which were constructed to serve a World War 2 airfield.

> **The Anthorn Radio Station antennae** were built in 1961 on top of a former three-runway World War 2 Royal Navy Air Station – HMS Nuthatch. The antennae have served as part of NATO's early warning defences and are still in operation for submarine communications.

The peculiar large brick World War 2 Anthorn firing butts were used to calibrate aircraft machine guns.

The road climbs steadily around the gorse covered headland to the tiny farming settlement of **Cardurnock**; a western extension to Hadrian's Wall once passed through here and archaeologists have located Mile Fortlets 4 and 5 just to its north. ◄

The road eventually arcs back eastwards where often wind-assisted cycling quickly brings into view **Bowness-on-Solway** and a sign that marks the start of Hadrian's Wall. The distance on the sign to Wallsend denotes going via the hiking route rather than the far less direct HCW.

From the 'to Rome' sign, a short fairly steep hill leads to the centre of the village and reveals the Roman military decision to build a fort here. Continue downhill to follow the coastline east; in very high tides this stretch can be subject to tidal flooding – although this is rare. Beneath your wheels, the remnants of both the Wall and Vallum – an earthwork that was a subsidiary part of the Wall's defences – are criss-crossed several times, while in adjacent fields the remains of various Roman milecastles, turrets and fortlets lie hidden beneath the earth.

*Only 1150 miles to Rome: Hadrian's Wall
begins at Bowness-on-Solway*

BOWNESS-ON-SOLWAY

The village of Bowness is situated on the site of the Roman Fort Miai – although little remains of the fort, it was one of the largest on Hadrian's Wall.

Looking back west from the sign to Rome at Bowness, it is possible to see the remaining stanchions of the Solway Viaduct – part of Solway Railway Junction opened in 1870. The viaduct once crossed the firth to connect to Annan in Scotland. On Sundays, Scots were known to walk across the bridge in order to take advantage of more liberal English alcohol laws. Reputedly there were incidences of returning inebriated souls falling off the viaduct to their deaths. The bridge proved costly to repair, being battered by tides and even ice floes in harsh winters; it was closed and dismantled in 1933.

Bowness has a super little pub – the King's Arms (open daily from 12pm). The village also has two cafés and public toilets in the village hall located immediately behind the pub. This has a completers' book for Hadrian's Wall Path and information boards, including one that acknowledges the ancient tradition of haaf netting. Haaf netting is still practised by local fisherman looking to catch salmon and trout in the Solway Firth. Its future is threatened by bird conservation projects that are unconcerned about dismantling traditional and sustainable livelihoods that have existed for centuries.

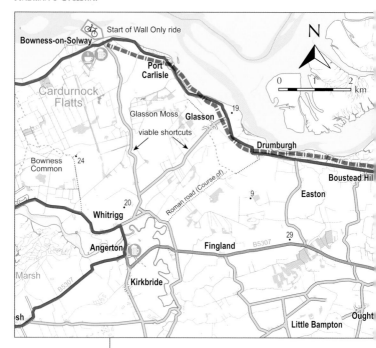

Port Carlisle was once connected to Carlisle by canal and rail.

The intriguingly named **Port Carlisle** is reached after a mile; its former quay spottable just off the coast. ◄ From Port Carlisle, continue straight along the coast road for two miles on a less distinctive stretch with occasional gentle inclines to reach **Drumburgh**.

Drumburgh Castle is a large defensive residence on the right at the east end of the village, which dates from 1307. Much of its stone was appropriated from the remains of Hadrian's Wall.

After Drumburgh a superb straight stretch crossing Easton and Burgh marshes is bordered on the right by the remains of a dismantled railway and canal, while to the left is the former line of the Wall.

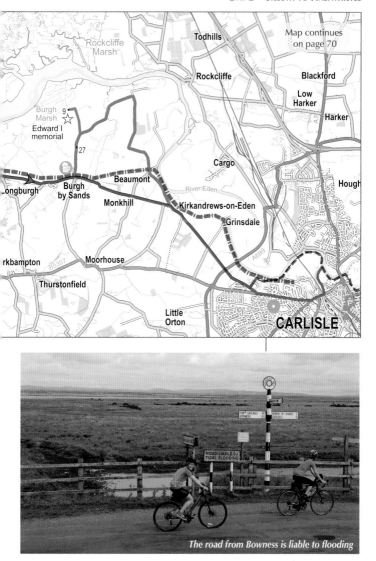

Map continues on page 70

The road from Bowness is liable to flooding

Burgh Marsh is the location of a famous UFO sighting – the Solway Firth Spaceman photo of 1964. A photo of five-year-old Elizabeth Templeton holding flowers, taken by her father, Jim, appears to show a strange spaceman in the background. The Templeton family did not see any other figures on the marsh at the time and were stunned by the photo when it came back from the developer's. Suggestions have been made – including in a reconstruction on the BBC's *The One Show* – to explain the figure as being Mrs Templeton accidentally walking into shot. This explanation seems stretched and the photo remains an intriguing mystery.

Continue straight ahead to meet the **Burgh by Sands** sign a significant distance before the village. The village has grown in a linear fashion clinging to the road and is stretched out. Next to the Greyhound Pub is a statue of Edward I – who died nearby on the Solway. After passing the statue, the road rises to a crossroads in 400m. Straight on is the standard HCW, while a left turn accesses the signed alternative HCW loop that incorporates the

'Beware the Hammer of the Scots' – passing the Edward I statue at Burgh by Sands

68

Edward I Memorial on the Solway. Note: at the time of writing, the sign that should be pointing back towards Bowness for east–west travellers has bent round the post and instead points rightwards – ignore it (it was too stiff for us to correct).

Alternative loop to Edward I memorial

The monument's setting upon a broad expanse of marsh and sands is memorable, but this is hardly a necessary diversion and time would be better spent allotted to Hadrian's Wall. A detour to view the Edward I monument adds two road miles to the overall HCW distance, while getting to the monument is on an off-road spur that adds yet another overall mile.

Turn left at the crossroads and follow the narrow road out of the village. After ¾ mile take a track left off a bend (essentially straight on) to a notice board. The monument can now be seen on the marsh sands in the distance. A track and path can be followed to its foot.

> The **Edward I memorial** claims to mark the exact spot where the king died. Over the centuries the Solway Firth has seen both English and Scottish armies making forays north and south while at the mercy of tides and risky terrain. Edward I (aka 'Longshanks' or 'Hammer of the Scots') died here on one such excursion in 1307. Although the scene befits a king in armour being struck down in the cut and thrust of battle, Edward died more prosaically of dysentery.

Return to the road and continue to follow the loop. At the village of **Beaumont**, turn right at the green for 50m then take a left opposite the church to **Kirkandrews-on-Eden**. At the T-junction, turn left to rejoin HCW.

Edward I memorial

Main route continues

From **Burgh by Sands**, continue due east, passing through **Monkhill** (pub – Drover's Rest) and **Kirkandrews-on-Eden**. Half a mile after Kirkandrews, a kink in the road creates a blind bend over the former railway bridge that requires care. At the large roundabout on Carlisle's outer northern ring road, use the cycle paths and crossings to facilitate safe passage directly across.

TRAVERSING CARLISLE

Cycling through Carlisle requires careful map reading as there are two options. The original HCW option is best and is described as the main route. It was well-signed before being closed due to flood repairs in 2015. Although it has reopened, it has not yet received replacement cycling signage. The alternative is well-signed as the '72', but is a less than ideal approach that is best avoided – especially in busy periods.

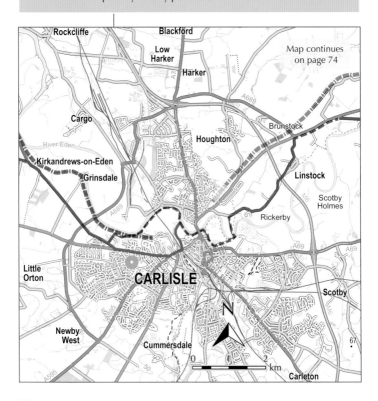

Map continues on page 74

Carlisle Castle

CARLISLE

Carlisle was known as *Luguvalium* by the Romans, who constructed a fort there probably as early as AD73 on the site of present day Carlisle Castle. Reputedly much of the city, like Rome, burned down under the reign of Nero – who was presumably playing his apocryphal fiddle. Carlisle was a Roman stronghold and formed a key base for the construction of Hadrian's Wall.

As a border town, Carlisle has an especially rich history dating from Roman times to the present day. Associated with the Border Reivers, the city was cursed by a Scottish Archbishop in 1525 and for the Millennium celebrations the council thought it would be a good idea to have the curse carved onto a granite boulder for an artwork. Many blamed the carving for the city's post-millennial flooding – which definitely had nothing at all to do with changing climate or poor river management! The stone can be seen in an underpass by the castle.

Carlisle was the birthplace and childhood home of US President Woodrow Wilson's mother, Janet. Her son, who oversaw American entry into World War 1 and was fundamental in establishing the forerunner to the United Nations with the ill-fated League of Nations in 1920, was fond of returning to his roots and visiting Carlisle. A pub in the city centre bears his name.

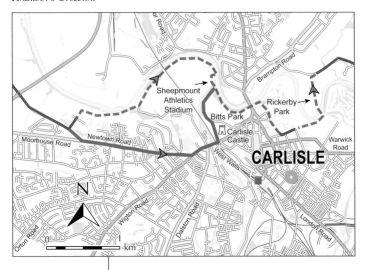

Recommended route through Carlisle

Cross the roundabout and head towards **Carlisle** on Burgh Road – there is 400m of segregated contra-flow cycle path on the right-hand side to make use of until the traffic calmed urban area starts. Once you reach housing, take the first available left onto Marconi Road. Follow this downhill towards the Burgh Industrial Estate to a T-junction. Diagonally right across from the T-junction is a fairly hard-to-spot footpath between the warehouses; it has steel tubular barriers to prevent motorcycle access. Head down this – the path is at times unsurfaced, but will cause no difficulties for road bikes. Continue on HCW until you spot Hadrian's Wall Path (National Trail) through the trees running parallel with the river; join it on the left close to a grassy clearing. Trend rightwards once on this to access the riverside down some stone steps with a metal handrail (tricky for heavily-laden cycle tourers). Dip under a former railway bridge. (If you have reached a hill with railway sleeper steps going up steeply, you have missed the river access by about 30m.) Follow Hadrian's Wall Path as it arcs beside the river to **Sheepmount Athletics Stadium**.

Head through the car park but take an immediate left after a small bridge to continue on Hadrian's Wall Path into **Bitts Park** (the alternative joins here). Carlisle Castle is also easily reached from this point.

Alternative route through Carlisle

This route is not recommended, unless you're particularly heavily loaded. From the roundabout, continue straight into Carlisle. Where Burgh Road reaches the B5307 take a shallow left. Carry on to a large roundabout on the A595 outside the McVitie's factory. Turn left towards the city centre, taking advantage of Carlisle's system of shared-use pavements. The road rises, crossing the River Caldew and West Coast Mainline. Just as you reach the red sandstone perimeter wall of **Carlisle Castle**, take a left down the minor Dacre Road. As this curves behind the castle, turn left onto Mayor's Drive to meet the primary route at a bridge near the **Sheepmount Athletics Stadium** car park. Follow the 72 rightwards (east) through the trees into **Bitts Park**.

Where the routes converge in Bitts Park, stay on the left with the river and take a left fork as the main road comes into view, then pass beneath a road bridge. You'll soon reach the Turf Tavern; continue straight on to meet a T-junction. Turn left onto a shared use path leading to Strand Road. At the end of this, head straight on to another cycle path. This path will soon join the river at a kink – bear rightwards. At the next fork, bear left to cross Memorial Bridge, with its ornate fish gate, into **Rickerby Park** – which surprisingly has cattle grazing in summer months. Follow the cycle path directly to the enormous white cenotaph.

> **Rickerby Park** was purchased as a site for the impressive granite war memorial built in 1922. The Border regiment, based at Carlisle Castle, lost more than 6,000 troops during World War 1.

At the T-junction, turn right to discover you've left Carlisle behind. ▶

The peculiarly named George Head Head's octagonal Victorian folly in the form of a peel tower can be seen in fields just after leaving Rickerby Park.

Gargoyle near the Eden Golf Club tearoom

Soon you'll cross the M6. After passing through the village of **Linstock**, you'll reach the busy A689 at a roundabout. Take a segregated contra-flow cycle path on the right. The proximity of the road nonetheless makes this one of the worst passages of the entire ride – it is soon over. At **Crosby-on-Eden** take the first right after the Stag Inn onto quieter roads. In a mile, the entrance drive to **Eden Golf Club** (good café, open to cyclists) is passed.

At **Newby East**, turn right and soon you'll cross the narrow Newby Bridge. Take an easily missed sharp left turn followed by an impish hill immediately after the Otter Inn (formerly the Haywain Inn) on the outskirts of **Warwick Bridge**.

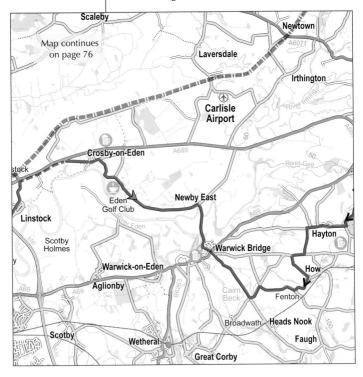

Map continues on page 76

Take care going directly across the busy A69. Roughly a mile later, take a left turn towards Fenton and How. This is soon after followed by a right turn leading to Fenton. In **Fenton**, turn left to eventually find a pleasant climb up to **How**, where an immediate left back downhill makes you wonder what was the purpose of the How excursion. Descend How Lane to a T-junction. Turn right then take the next left to the pleasant village of **Hayton**.

On the narrow Newby Bridge

On the left after the Stone Inn is Walnut Field with its impressive walnut tree. The magnificent slightly hollowed **Hayton Walnut Tree** is claimed to be one of the 30 broadest trees in the UK and was reputedly planted in 1539, during the reign of Henry VIII.

Continue up from Hayton to a T-junction at the hamlet of Townhead, where you should take a left before soon encountering a taxing hill climb. A pleasant fast section intervenes before care is needed on a steep descent with a blind bend down to Low Gelt Bridge. Turn right

75

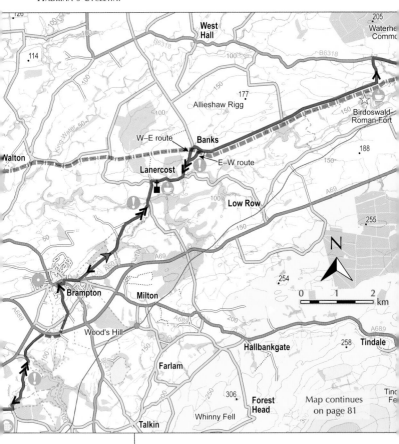

to cross the bridge then follow the dead end road to its termination. Here, you'll join a cycle path that has a 72 signpost promising it is 70¾ miles to Newcastle. Pass through a tunnel under the busy A69, then take a right at the T-junction. A left turn onto Gelt Road soon follows that leads downhill to **Brampton** high street where a right turn leads to the market square, which disappointingly functions as a car park, while a left leads past a statue of Hadrian at the junction of the A6071.

Brampton dates from the 7th century, although a statue erected in 1999 of Emperor Hadrian imagines an earlier history with the young Roman passing hereabouts. During the reign of Henry III in 1252 Brampton was awarded a market by royal charter on Wednesdays. The town had a role to play in Bonnie Prince Charlie's Jacobite rebellion of 1745, and Charlie briefly made his headquarters here. The Capon Tree Monument marks the spot where six Jacobite rebels were 'hung, drawn and quartered' in 1746 after having been dragged through the streets. The monument is located at the western end of Capon Tree Road.

In the market square, turn left before the distinctive octagonal visitor centre. Then turn right on a traffic calmed stretch of the A6071 for 200m over the brow of a hill where a left turn by a green will take you away from the town.

The climb out of Brampton up the Swartle makes for pleasant and steady enough riding, yet a sense that

Emperor Hadrian, Brampton

The distinctive red sandstone of Lanercost Priory

a great Pennines traverse has truly begun soon becomes apparent. After a mile, you'll have a steep descent to **Lanercost Priory** (café).

> The Augustinian **Lanercost Priory** was founded around 1169. Like many buildings in the proximity of Hadrian's Wall, the Wall was raided to provide much of its stone and Roman carvings can be seen on some of the stones in the Priory. In the winter of 1307 Edward I paid a visit to Lanercost on a journey north to 'hammer' the Scots, but falling ill and needing to recuperate, stayed three months and proved an expensive guest. During the Dissolution, an inventory listed the church as housing a prized relic of Christendom – St Mary Magdelene's girdle; sadly it has since been lost. There is a fee to visit the priory, but not the church.

Follow the road round Lanercost Priory and settle into a tame mile of the Irthing Valley that gives little hint of the imminent tough climb up to Banks. A mile after the priory, the road bends leftwards and the climb to Banks begins – this is both testing and superb, peaking at 1 in 6. The village sign for Banks seems cruelly placed to get cyclists' hopes up of an imminent cessation to the gradient – it is quite some distance below the village and the top of the hill! The W–E route on the hill takes a slightly different line to the E–W route: turn left along a shaded road then take the first right to rejoin the direct route with a left turn. The climb eases as the village green is reached and Hadrian's Wall pops up as a reward for efforts and a neat little surprise on a flat section shortly after – it is a good spot for a well-deserved rest. Milecastle 53 is hidden under a house at **Banks**. ◀

The remains seen after the village are an intermediary turret, 52A.

After Banks comes the finest three-mile stretch of riding on the conventional HCW – this is especially so on weekdays during term time when there are very few vehicles around. Continue due east on the road, which retains its elevated position above the Irthing Valley and passes numerous easily seen remnants of the Wall.

Topping out with the surprise appearance of the Wall above Banks

BIRDOSWALD ROMAN FORT

Birdoswald Roman Fort can largely be seen from the perimeter fence, however, it is only when entering the site that the precipitous drops on its south side can be realised. These emphasise the dramatic situation of the fort and also reveal the horn-shaped bend of the River Irthing that gave the fort its Celtic name, *Banna*, which means 'horn'. A comparison between the model of the fort in Roman times with how it is today reveals the startling encroachment of the River Irthing and how the escarpment has moved nearly 100m closer since Roman times. The sheering away of the escarpment seems to be as much the work of rainwater seeping into fissures in the boulder clay left by the Romans and, more recently, by archaeologists, as it is the work of the river.

Partly because of the erosion, excavation of a Roman military cemetery began in 1999. This was the subject of an episode of Channel Four's *Time Team* (S07-E05) that turns up the first Roman burial urn found along the Wall. Although a fortified bastle house stood on the site during the time of the Border Reivers, the mock Medieval building that houses the museum dates from the Victorian era; its owner loved the fort so much he named his son 'Oswald'.

Passing the 12th-century Thirlwall Castle

The courtyard at Birdoswald Roman Fort has a café open to the public with adjoining toilets and an out tap for refilling water bottles.

The 12th-century Thirlwall Castle is supposedly haunted by a demonic black dwarf who guards a hidden golden table; you have been warned…or tempted.

In three delightful miles, you'll reach the **Roman Fort of Birdoswald**. ◄

The first bend on the downhill from Birdoswald allows an iconic view of Hadrian's Wall as it stretches off to the distant Walltown Crags. At the T-junction, turn right downhill on the B6318 to **Gilsland**, where you'll cross the River Irthing once more. A mile after Gilsland, take a left turn down into Longbyre – there can be a little loose gravel here. A further left leads you over a level crossing to a gated cycle path on the right. This proves a pleasant passage enhanced by the nearby Thirlwall Castle. ◄

Cross the Tipalt Burn by a bridge (or a tricky ford if you're daring) and follow the the unsurfaced road to a T-junction in **Greenhead** where there is an excellent café on the right.

It is now time to prepare yourself for the toughest climb of the entire HCW – Greenwhelt Bank. This peaks at around 1 in 4 near its entry and the segregated cycle path is a little too narrow to allow much zig-zagging if you're heavily loaded. Turn left and after 100m look out for a tricky left turn off the road onto the cycle path. After the cycle path flattens out, a junction with a minor road near the **Roman Army Museum** is reached.

The **Roman Army Museum** at Greenhead is situated on the site of Carvoran Roman fort (also known as Magna). Few earthworks remain, but the museum is well worth a visit to give context to the Wall and Roman occupation of the area. The museum's interactive displays and 3D films bring the Wall to life and are aimed less at knowledgeable antiquarians than at younger visitors and those looking for a superb introduction to the history of the Wall. The café and toilets are for museum visitors only and

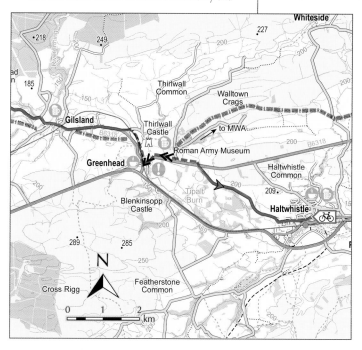

the site is partnered with Vindolanda (joint entrance tickets are available). Walltown Crags are a good place to see the Wall and are easily reached by heading to the car park with public toilets and bicycle rails 100m further along the road.

SEVERAL OPTIONS NOW PRESENT THEMSELVES:

- If you're sticking to the official route of HCW, follow the main route description to Haltwhistle.

- You may, however, decide to leave the official HCW at this point and adopt the unsigned MWA (see Day 2A). Although we are generally route purists, in this instance we strongly recommend doing the MWA. The MWA massively enhances the experience of HCW by maintaining cycling on the high tops in the proximity of the Wall and allowing access to some of the Wall's most iconic sections along the Whin Sill geological feature. The MWA bypasses the unexceptional Haltwhistle, the ensuing valley floor ride to Barden Mill and a further protracted climb. It rejoins the official route just before Vindolanda Roman Fort.

- If you're camping at Herding Hill Farm, Hadrian's Wall Campsite or Winshields Farm Campsite, the descent to Haltwhistle might prove a little excessive. After all, all height lost to the south Tyne valley will only need to be immediately regained. Continuing on the B6318 to those campsites is a shortcut option (although using the MWA described in Day 2A would be better). It is worth pointing out that the B6318 requires much caution, especially where it has hidden dips and you will not wish to be on it for very long.

If you're continuing on HCW to **Haltwhistle**, cross over the minor road onto a briefly unsurfaced stretch of path. At its end, cross the B6318 and make a 2½ mile minor road descent to a T-junction, where you should take a left turn and carry on to the centre of town and – as is claimed – the centre of Britain.

HALTWHISTLE

Haltwhistle, although fairly unremarkable, claims to be the centre of Great Britain. As always with such claims, a degree of imagination is needed and the measurement appears to have defined Britain's northern limit as being on the Orkney Islands. Nonetheless, there is a plate and badge embedded in the small market square to commemorate this geographical novelty. Haltwhistle presently

Haltwhistle – the centre of Britain

has plenty of cafés and restaurants but no bakery. Those eager for that cycle-tourer staple 'pie power' will find that the sandwich shop on the left approaching the market square does excellent hot homemade pies and giant scones that could feed an entire Roman Army.

EAST TO WEST

Unless on the MWA, a gradual climb is needed to regain the tops from Haltwhistle, although much of this height is lost quickly down the steep and awkward Greenwhelt Bank. The climb to Birdoswald is not too challenging, although it has a steep and satisfying bend as the Wall is reached. At Banks the E–W and W–E routes momentarily split on the descent, with the E–W option continuing straight on and requiring care to be taken with blind bends. While the climbs from Lanercost over the Swartle and up Gelt Road from Brampton are both tough, the hardest climb of the day is that which goes from the River Gelt just after Brampton. This has a steep entry followed by a long drag to its summit – the road is at least quiet. The escape from the river cycle paths at Carlisle should not be difficult as long as the route is followed until the unmistakable stone steps under the viaduct can be used.

DAY 2A
More Wall Alternative

Start	Top of Greenwhelt Bank, at turning for Roman Army Museum
Finish	Turning for Vindolanda, beyond Once Brewed
Distance	10.2 miles (16.5km)
Total ascent	300m
Steepest climb	Hound Hill and Steel Rigg
Terrain	Predominantly on minor roads. A 1.1km off-road section after the hamlet of Walltown has 300m of very bumpy terrain (challenging for road bikes); an on-road alternative is described.
OS maps	OL43
Refreshments	Twice Brewed Inn, Once Brewed

This route is strongly recommended – especially if you're visiting Hadrian's Wall for the first time. The MWA is neither a shortcut nor an elongation: if it is adopted, the overall height gain and distance of the ride is the same as on the conventional HCW. As good as HCW is, the Sustrans route has a significant drawback in missing some of the most iconic sections of the Wall. The MWA eschews a needless descent to Haltwhistle and a fairly forgettable valley ride in favour of visiting some of the finest parts of Hadrian's Wall and enabling more riding on high ground in view of the Whin Sill – the stunning geological feature with which the wall is most associated. It involves 1km of unsurfaced track cycling that has been ridden with care by one of the authors on a road bike, but there is little doubt it stretches a road bike to its limits. (It would be a shame to miss this fantastic unsurfaced section, but this part can be bypassed by using the less-than-ideal B6318.) Refer also to Seeing more of the Wall in the Introduction.

Turn left on the minor road to the **Roman Army Museum** and, more or less opposite its entrance, turn right onto a dead end road signed to 'Hadrian's Wall – Walltown Crags'. This leads you through woods and draws close to **Walltown Crags**.

Signed footpaths on the left can be taken to explore the Wall at **Walltown Crags**. The simplest of these leaves a small parking area as the woods end, although a track uphill from the farming hamlet of Walltown to Walltown Gap between Milecastle 45 (left) and Turret 44B (right) is also straightforward.

At Walltown the tarmac deteriorates and the road surface is generally caked in farming detritus. Continue for 500m. Just after passing a magnificent lime kiln ignore the sharp left uphill to **Alloa Lea Farm** and instead head straight on to pass through a gate and follow an unsurfaced track. Although admittedly very awkward, many will find this track offers some of the most memorable cycling on the three-day tour. The first 300m are the most uneven. Follow the track as it curves around a knoll and crosses the Roman Vallum ditch, where mud may force

The Wall atop Windshield Crags

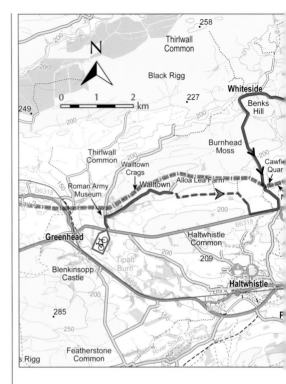

you to momentarily dismount. The track improves after the cattle grid and follows a superb raised section that uses part of the Roman turf structure of the Vallum.

The views towards **Windshields Crags** – the highest point of the Wall – from the raised track above the Vallum are magnificent. The Whin Sill is the shapely escarpment of rock over which the scenic middle section of Hadrian's Wall runs. It provided an obvious natural defence and vantage point. The Sill was formed by magma from tectonic shift nearly 300 million years ago.

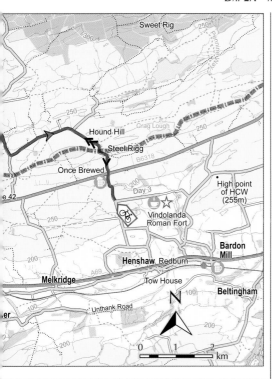

Sweet Rig

Hound Hill

Steel Rigg

Once Brewed

Crag Lough

B6318

Day 3

High point
of HCW
(255m)

e 42

Vindolanda
Roman Fort

Bardon
Mill

Henshaw Redburn

Melkridge

Tow House

Beltingham

Unthank Road

N

0   1   2
km

*Cawfield Quarry
by Milecastle 42 is
a designated dark
skies site and ideal
for stargazers*

The adjoining car park at Cawfield Quarry has public toilets and bicycle railings.

After 800m, you'll reach a tarmac road. Follow it through a gate to a junction with the B6318. Turn left onto the B6318: this stretch is straight with no hidden dips, but still requires care. In 800m, turn left opposite the Milecastle Inn towards Cawfield Crags and Milecastle 42. **Milecastle 42** is impressively situated and well worth a visit. ◄

Follow the road past Cawfield Crags car park, then make a testing climb to overcome **Burnhead Moss**. The road swings around **Benks Hill** in a tremendous setting then trends eastward onto a gated section. Turn right at the T-junction after the cattle grid. The vantage of the road now allows the natural defences of the Whin Sill to be fully appreciated. Turn left in 1 mile (signed 'Twice Brewed 2¼ miles'). Follow the road as it climbs,

Sycamore Gap

gradually at first, before a couple of tough inclines are needed to overcome **Hound Hill** and the high point of the MWA at 294m. The **Steel Rigg** car park shortly afterwards signals the end of the climbing; a stop here to explore the Wall is strongly recommended (refer to Seeing more of the Wall in the Introduction).

Nestled comfortably in a scenic nick of the Wall, the tree at **Sycamore Gap** is the most photographed tree in Northumberland. It may be familiar from a fight scene in the film *Robin Hood Prince of Thieves*. Robin claims the tree as his own in the film, and saves a boy who hides from deerhounds in it. Kevin Costner and Morgan Freeman discuss mistletoe picked from the tree and the ways of love. The tree's exact age is not known, although it is probably a few hundred years old.

From the brow of Steel Rigg, head downhill to a crossroads at **Once Brewed** where the giant Sill YHA and Twice Brewed pub will be seen across the road. Cross the B6318 onto the minor road opposite and follow this for 700m, then take a left turn downhill to Vindolanda to rejoin the official HCW.

ONCE BREWED AND TWICE BREWED

The scattered hamlet of Once Brewed, the popular Sill YHA and the Twice Brewed pub are on the MWA. The hamlet is somewhat eccentrically named as Once Brewed on road signs coming from the east but as Twice Brewed for those arriving from the west. The Twice Brewed name is sometimes said to have originated from Yorkist soldiers on the eve of the Battle of Hexham who demanded stronger 'twice brewed' ale to give them courage to face down the Lancastrians. Whatever the story, ale has been brewed on the premises for more than 500 years.

DAY 3
Haltwhistle to South Shields

Start	Haltwhistle (NY 705 640)
Alternative start	Once Brewed if using the MWA (NY 752 668)
Finish	Arbeia Roman Fort, South Shields (NZ 364 680)
Alternative finish	Tynemouth (NZ 372 692)
Distance	57 miles (89km)
Total ascent	953m
Steepest climb	The climb up from Vindolanda to the high point of the route. This has a wickedly steep entry at around 1 in 5, although this is short-lived and the hill thereafter is more gradual and amenable.
Terrain	Minor roads through the remaining hilly Pennines, followed by protracted valley cycling. The final 24 miles of the route to and through Newcastle are nearly all on cycle paths.
OS maps	OL43, 316
Refreshments	Vindolanda (café, entry fee); Bardon Mill (tea room and pub); Newbrough (pub); Chesters Roman Fort just off route (good café, entry fee); Bridge End (Boatside Inn); Hexham (Café Enna, Tynedale Golf Club); Corbridge; Prudhoe (Tyne Riverside Country Park Café); Newburn Ford (café and pub); Newcastle quayside
Intermediate distances	Vindolanda, 8 miles; Newbrough, 15 miles; Hexham, 22 miles; Corbridge, 26 miles; Prudhoe, 33 miles; Tyne Bridge quayside, 45 miles; Wallsend, 50 miles; South Shields, 57 miles
Note	If you miss the ferry at South Shields, you will either need to divert through the Tyne Cycle and Pedestrian Tunnel or adopt the Tynemouth alternative ending

This day's riding involves a climb to Vindolanda – probably the most famous of the forts on Hadrian's Wall – and beyond it the highest point of HCW. An exceptional gradual descent leads to the villages of Newbrough and Fourstones. One last substantial climb is made to leave the South Tyne River in favour of its northern sister, where Chesters Roman Fort can be easily reached by a brief spur. The Tyne Valley is then followed through Hexham and Corbridge – the latter of these is the site of another Roman settlement. At Prudhoe the superb shared use Tyne Riverside Path is adopted. This makes for very pleasant easy riding, predominantly on former railways, towards Newcastle. There is probably no better city cycle network in the UK than in Newcastle upon Tyne. Nonetheless, some sections on shared use paths in the proximity of busy roads do mar the route where HWC is joined by the original C2C. Things recover on the Quayside Path that passes beneath the iconic Tyne Bridge. Cycle paths then predominate to the culmination of Hadrian's Wall at Segedunum in Wallsend. Thereafter further cycle paths and minor road connections lead without complication to the Tyne Ferry Terminal (**early service finish on Sundays**, see description for times). A delightful and scenic crossing of the historic Tyne by ferry leaves only a few minutes more cycling to reach the end of HCW at Arbeia Roman Fort – although a descent to the beach is a somewhat mandatory second ending.

From the centre of Haltwhistle, follow the high street eastwards with a steep descent to a T-Junction at the broad B6322. Take care crossing this to join a road more or less opposite that swings leftwards under the A69 and along the South Tyne Valley. This proves a flattish interlude between the route's bigger hill climbs, passing

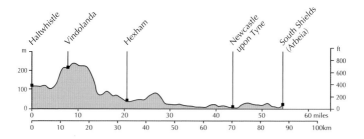

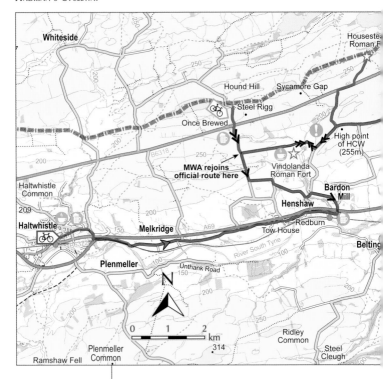

through **Melkridge** and the Henshaw-Redburn conurbation to reach **Bardon Mill**.

> **Bardon Mill** is a good destination for an overnight stop if you're looking for somewhere a little quieter and smaller than Haltwhistle. The village has one pub, the Bowes Hotel, a village store and tea room, and is served by the Tyne Valley Railway.

At the eastern end of Bardon Mill, take a left turn opposite the war memorial to commence the climb to Vindolanda. Pass under the A69 and follow the road as it eventually swings round to the west and essentially

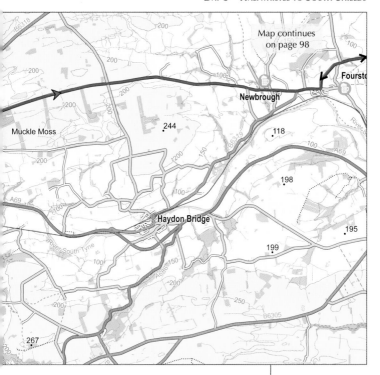

doubles back on a portion of the day's eastwards pro-
gress. At the crossroads in Westwood, take an unlikely
left turn down the hill. The road crosses a bridge over
Chainly Burn, after which you need to take the first
right turn uphill signed to Vindolanda. The climbing
is gradual, but fairly prolonged and goes up in two
long stages that can be affected by strong westerlies.
At the T-junction turn right. After a flat section with a
slight descent, take a right turn beside a line of pines
to commence the free-wheeling delight of the straight
Stanegate Roman Road to **Vindolanda Roman Fort**. The
famous Sycamore Gap can be spotted in the distance
just after the pines. ▶

The More Wall
Alternative rejoins
the route at the
line of pines.

Cyclists approaching Vindolanda with Sycamore Gap beyond

VINDOLANDA

Archaeologist on an active dig at Vindolanda

Vindolanda is arguably the most famous Roman Fort in Britain and a good choice for a stop. The site is privately owned and has an £8 entry fee, although for that price there is much to explore and take in. While a lot of the fort can be seen at a distance from the perimeter fence, including a reconstruction of what Hadrian's Wall would have been like in Roman times, it is only once inside Vindolanda that the fort's scale can be realised.

Walking along the narrow streets there is a hint of Pompeii about the place. The museum, like the café, is hidden in a dip in the woods. It is particularly impressive and among its large collection contains a skull – apparently belonging to a local Briton that the Romans appear to have placed on a spike as a warning to other 'barbarians'. Vindolanda remains a site of active archaeological digs; wheelbarrows and painstaking mud-scraping are not uncommon sights. The café (in a mock-Roman style) and the toilets cannot be accessed without paying the entrance fee. The 18th-century Causeway House before Vindolanda is the only building in Northumberland still thatched in heather – traditionally known as 'black thack'. It can be rented by groups of four.

Alternative to Steel Rigg

It is better to add a spur to the main route and take the time and energy to visit Steel Rigg where a pleasant hike allows you to see the Wall in its most famous locations (see Seeing more of the Wall and the More Wall Alternative in Day 2A). To reach Steel Rigg, continue uphill on National Cycle Route 68 for 700m. Take care crossing directly over the B6318, and follow the minor road for 800m steeply uphill to the **Steel Rigg** car park (bike rails).

The mysterious thin watchman above the route on the Barcombe Moor is Long Stone; little is known of its origins.

From **Vindolanda**, with its distance to Rome sign, prepare for the hardest climb of the day and head steeply downhill to cross the burn. The hill rises steeply and its gradient peaks early at 1 in 5; it is a beast easily tamed, however. At the minor T-junction, turn left and follow the road round the hillside to the **highest point of HCW** (255m), commemorated by a signpost. ◄

Detour to Housesteads Roman Fort

Housesteads can be reached by a moderately short spur from HCW: turn left on a minor road above Vindolanda where a lime kiln can be seen from the junction and is passed in 50m. At the B6318 turn right for 1300m to reach the visitor centre and café or, better, after 400m use the gated tarmac road with pedestrian right of way that leads directly to the museum and fort on the hillside.

> **Housesteads Roman Fort** is overseen by English Heritage and the National Trust (£9 entrance fee, free to members). It is perhaps the most romantically situated of all the Wall settlements, on a lofty stretch of the Wall that requires a spot of hiking to be reached. The fort was unusual in not having a running water source and being reliant on the plentiful Northumbrian rainwater instead. The setting is the real attraction here, but notable parts of the site are the particularly well-preserved granaries and reputedly the best examples of Roman latrines in Britain.

*Latrines at glorious
Housesteads*

From the high point of HCW, a superb stretch of road in an elevated position allows the splendour of the northern Pennines to be fully appreciated. Continue, noting that your wheels are spinning once more over the Stanegate Roman road; Hadrian's Wall forms the skyline to the north and Gindon Lough is a distinct feature on the left. The road soon coalesces into a pleasurably protracted effortless descent to **Newbrough**, which bills itself as 'Gateway to the Northumberland National Park'. (Newbrough has a pub, the Red Lion.) Continue cycling to reach **Fourstones**, which has a country store at the filling station. ▸

Fourstones boasts one of more than 4000 crows' nest beacons spread across the Commonwealth to commemorate the Queen's Golden Jubilee in 2002.

97

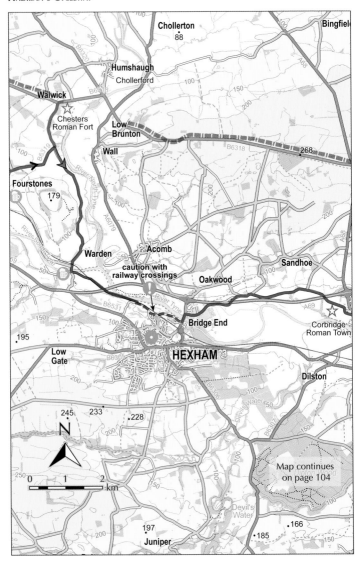

From Fourstones, HCW makes a significant detour in search of quieter roads and also to draw the route close enough to facilitate a visit to Chesters Roman Fort. The ascent over Whinny Hill – the last substantial climb of the route – may seem illogical on paper but is definitely worth sticking to. Just after you pass the green wooden church of St Aidan's, take a left in Fourstones onto the quiet B6319 and climb steadily to the top.

From the crest of Whinny Hill descend for a mile to a signed right turn.

Detour to Chesters Roman Fort
If planning to visit Chesters Roman Fort, ignore the right signed turning and continue for ¾ mile to where the entrance will be seen on the right.

> **Chesters Roman Fort** has a very relaxed feel and is well worth a visit (£4.50, free to English Heritage members). It is pleasantly situated on the North River Tyne and boasts one of the best preserved Roman bathhouses in Britain. It has a good café. The bijou Clayton Museum has all the artefacts crammed endearingly together, presumably as they have been since the Victorian era. A stone bust is labelled 'head of a bearded man' – the beard is obvious, make of the clarification what you will!

After visiting the fort, return to the main route by retracing the way you came.

Take the right turn onto a narrow minor road that runs parallel with the North Tyne River for a couple of miles before a brief climb and descent lead to the South Tyne River. This is met at Warden Bridge next to the Boatside Inn. Turn left, cross the bridge and take an immediate left down a dead end road. This eventually blends into an excellent cycle path running beside the Tyne Valley Railway. After a mile, take care as you cross the railway on foot (bicycles must be dismounted) – the trains are fast

The impressive bathhouse at Chesters

A number of rail crossings are encountered near Hexham

here; do not take any chances. Follow the narrow Spittal Lane eastwards to a playing field and housing estate on the fringe of **Hexham**.

Hexham is largely bypassed by HCW and feels like a busy industrialised town with little more than a sprawling complex of retail parks and few would fancy being enmeshed in its web. However, the centre of the old town is surprising and Hexham Abbey is well worth a short visit. The abbey is a beautiful place with a café and displays explaining its Roman connections. Chief among these is the fascinating tombstone of the Roman standard-bearer Flavius, which depicts him on horseback while a 'barbarian' – for 'barbarian', simply read local Briton – is being trampled underfoot. This carving should guard against putting too rosy a tint on the Roman occupation: the Roman presence in Britain was an act of invasion and subjugation by a continental foe that would cause – like

Tombstone of Flavius with 'barbarian' – read Briton – trampled underfoot

101

the later invading Vikings and Normans – massive and often brutal upheaval in the lives of ordinary Britons. The abbey crypt also houses several altars to Roman gods.

Just after the rail crossing, Café Enna at Tynedale Golf Club offers a convenient stop.

Follow the road round the playing field then go straight across at the minor junction. Pass a playground on your left and 50m beyond that, dismount for a gated railway crossing. ◄ A set of free public toilets can be found 100m or so beyond.

Follow the minor road beside the Tyne to emerge on a busy roundabout at the south side of Hexham Bridge (those wishing to visit the abbey should follow signs to the abbey from here). The HCW sign across the road can be confusing: it is intended to direct E–W riders to a tunnel under the bridge that avoids the roundabout. Take care cycling across the congested bridge – heavily loaded cyclists should locate the tunnel behind the boathouse and dismount to make use of the pavement on the east side of the bridge. Once you're across the river, take the first right onto Ferry Road. This valley road, the only alternative to the monster A69, can be a little busy. Follow it for three fairly indistinct miles to **Corbridge**.

CORBRIDGE

Corbridge has evolved from Coria – the most northerly settlement of the Roman Empire. Access to the remains of the supporting Roman settlement is on a signed right turn just before the town is reached (entrance fee £4, free to English Heritage members). Its small museum houses the Corbridge Hoard including Roman armour, weaponry and writing equipment. Archaeologists have established that the fort was largely burnt down in AD105 and 180–81 – possibly by invading or rebellious northerners. King John visited the site in 1204 in the hope of finding buried treasure to ease his debts. He did not and, after an attempt to tax the barons went awry, was forced to sign the Magna Carta in 1215.

In Corbridge, turn right at the T-junction. After the Wheatsheaf Inn and a bend, turn left on the one-way Hill Street (E–W riders should use Middle Street, which passes St Andrew's church and the market square). At the end of Hill Street, turn right, passing free public toilets, then take the next left and climb steadily out of town on the often busy B6530.

After 1½ miles, leave the B6530 with a right turn onto quieter fare (signed to Bywell).

The road then takes you between wheatfields and a forest plantation on your descent to the River Tyne. At the oddly configured crossroads, head straight on ready to take the next left turn before the road crosses the river. The minor Bywell Road makes for superb riding beside the Tyne. Shortly after a sneaky little 1 in 6 hill hidden by a bend turn right towards **Ovingham** (essentially the northern half of Prudhoe).

Coria Roman settlement at Corbridge

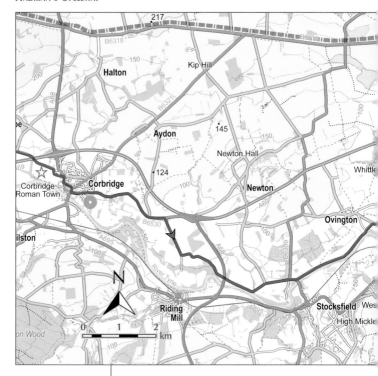

The impressive 11th-century **Prudhoe Castle**, visible above the town on the south side of the Tyne, has a claim to be the only significant Northumberland border castle to resist the Scots during centuries of border wars.

The western end of the four-mile long Tyne Riverside Country Park has a convenient café, and there are free public toilets to its rear.

Look out for a right turn downhill off a bend near Ovingham Village Hall. The narrow single lane Ovingham Bridge is best crossed by the adjacent wide pedestrian bridge. Across the river, turn immediately right into the Tyne Riverside Country Park. ◄

From near the café, turn right onto an excellent surfaced cycle path beside the Tyne, initially passing under

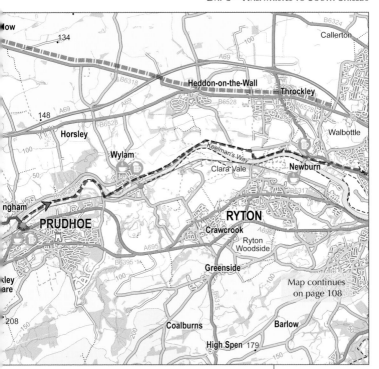

Map continues on page 108

the southern end of Ovingham Bridge before reaching the 'Prudhoe Spetchells' in a wooded area.

ICI had a chemical works in **Prudhoe** until the 1960s that produced explosives and fertiliser during World War 2. The incongruous giant chalk embankments now synonymous with the Spetchells Nature Reserve are reputedly a by-product of those processes – although suggestions that they might have been left in order to disguise the factory from German reconnaissance spies seem plausible. A variety of rare miner bees and other fauna make the Spetchells their home. The picturesque hexagonal

105

Hexagonal chimney of the Wylam Pumping Station

chimney across the Tyne from the Spetchells was part of the Wylam Pumping Station and dates back to the 1870s.

Follow the pleasant cycle path as it arcs with the river around the Hagg to meet the tiny settlement of Hagg Bank. Here, take a hidden left before a small bridge to access an awkward resumption of the cycle path. This now crosses the impressive disused Hagg Bank 'Railway' Bridge with its 73m span. ▶

Built in 1876 and regarded as the forerunner to the Tyne Bridge, the bridge's design ensured that no piers were dug into the riverbed, avoiding the fragile mine systems below.

Wylam Colliery was home to the world's first steam locomotive – the Puffing Billy, constructed in 1813–14. While the Puffing Billy is housed in the Science Museum in London, Wylam does boast the free bijou Wylam Railway Museum in Wylam library only 30m off route. Its opening times are limited to those of the library (Tuesday and Thursday afternoons and Saturday mornings). To access the museum: cross Hagg Bridge, pass beneath two road bridges and take a left turn doubling back for 30m to the red-bricked library.

The cycle path offers only minimum exposure to the urban area of **Wylam** and continues along a historic rail line for two miles to the eastern end of the Tyne Riverside Country Park. On the cycle path just after Wylam you'll pass a wonderful white cottage that is the birthplace of train and rail innovator George 'The Rocket' Stephenson.

On reaching a road, turn sharply right onto another cycle path towards the river. This joins Hadrian's Wall Path, which you should follow eastwards. A boat launch area is exited in the corner by the river. There is a café and public toilets set back away from the river here.

A memorial to the site of the **Battle of Newburn Ford** (1640) adjoins the car park just before Newburn. The battle saw the defeat of Charles I's forces by the Scots and set in motion a chain of events leading to the English Civil War.

Memorial for the Battle of Newburn Ford

After the pleasantly situated Boat House Pub, you'll meet a minor crossroads with traffic lights. Go straight across to an easily missed cycle path in the trees. This initially succeeds in avoiding the busy city roads of Newcastle, until you reach Neptune Road. After crossing this, Hadrian's Wall Path parts company with the cycle path.

The following section is easily the least enjoyable passage of the entire HCW. Head downhill on the shared use pavement on the left side of Neptune Road. Staying on the pavement, turn left to follow the path beside the busy road. After passing a large roundabout, it is necessary to use the crossing to join the shared-use pavement

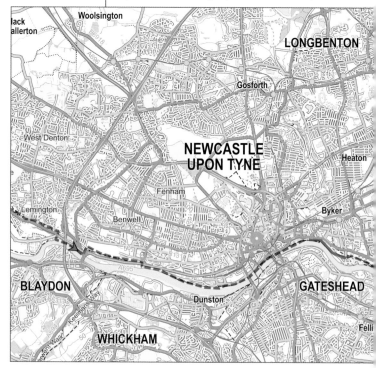

on the river side of the road. After a few hundred metres, at another dangerously busy roundabout use a crossing to return to the left side of the road. An escape is soon made leftwards onto a cycle path through playing fields and trees that offers about a mile of respite. When you reach the road once more, take advantage of the shared-use path for 100m or so before a pedestrian crossing takes you to the shared use path on the river side of the road. Follow this for an awful 300m, until you can make a rightwards escape along the pavement of the quieter William Armstrong Drive. After 200m or so the path becomes a dedicated segregated shared use cycle path beside the Tyne – thank goodness.

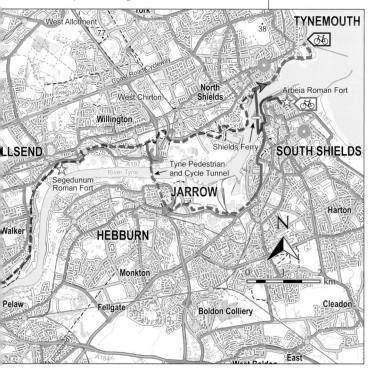

The Newcastle Quayside Path takes you into the heart of a cosmopolitan riverside area that is in turns vibrant and relaxing – many cycle tourers have been way-laid here on their way to the coast. Care can be needed with occasional blind turns, pedestrians and dog walkers – a bell is of great help. The route is not difficult to follow and passes beneath the Tyne Bridge in two miles.

The iconic **Tyne Bridge** was opened in 1928 and was built by the same company that designed the Sydney Harbour Bridge. The Tyne Bridge is probably on the same site as Pons Aelius – the first bridge built across the Tyne by the Romans in the second century to serve the Pons Aelius Roman Fort. It is worth venturing onto the impressive full tilt Gateshead Millennium pedestrian and cycle bridge for good views.

Continue along the north bank of the Tyne. The cycle path ceases after a quay is crossed near 'The Hub': a cycle hire shop, cycle mechanics and café that closes earlier than many running-late HCW and C2C finishers

Nearing Newcastle

would like – 4pm. Continue more conventionally on the left side of the surprisingly quiet former industrial riverside road. As the road forks, bear left gradually uphill and across a mini roundabout. Bear left at the peculiar Siamese-twin Merman sculpture and in 60m take a left turn onto a cycle path.

This raised cycle path is shared with Hadrian's Wall Path and follows a former rail line mostly through trees. It makes for pleasant quieter riding after the bustle of the quayside. There are five minor road crossings that interrupt the path before the **Segedunum Roman Fort** at **Wallsend**.

While reaching the Wall's end is a satisfying milestone, there are five intricately worked miles still to wheel until the journey's end can truly be called. These miles need diligent route finding. Continue along the segregated cycle path; in 500m a special arch commemorates

SEGEDUNUM ROMAN FORT

At Wallsend, an excavated section of Hadrian's Wall from the Segedunum Roman Fort is bisected by the cycle path. While this small section of wall is a little scruffy and invariably plagued by urban detritus – there is nonetheless something fascinating in seeing that its stone had been buried and not, over the centuries, entirely appropriated by urban developments. The stretch of wall that drops away from the path has a derelict office building on top of it and looks bizarre, although it is worth noting that it was only in the 1970s that the fort was – somewhat surprisingly – revealed during the clearance of Victorian terraced housing. Segedunum was constructed between AD122–127 as an eastern extension of Hadrian's Wall from the Pons Aelius Fort. Although the ruins can mostly be seen from the perimeter, a fee of £5.95 allows closer inspection and entrance to a museum and worthwhile viewing tower.

Sentius Tectonicus sculpture at Segedunum

HCW. The roundabout beyond is initially negotiated on the right, but while a cycle path continues on the right-hand side of the road, it is necessary to cross over to the shared use cycle path on the left side of the road. This parts company with the road completely by slipping leftwards downhill beside the Willington Viaduct where there are slightly different winding lines for uphill and downhill cyclists. Turn right on reaching Ropery Lane, but take a left after 50m or so onto a cyclepath that sneaks past a small industrial estate.

The path emerges on Armstrong Road, which you follow to its conclusion (**the Running late alternative route diverges here** – see end of Day 3 route description).

Turn left to follow the road round to the next junction where a left turn uphill is followed immediately by a right turn at a toucan crossing onto a cycle path. This weaves a little circuitously but brilliantly to cross a bridge where the Tyne Road Tunnel toll booths will be seen. A first roundabout is largely negotiated by a cut-through cycle path. At a third roundabout, take a right turn still on the shared use pavement down Coble Dean at the Royal Quays. Look out for a left turn using a toucan crossing to a cycle path hidden in trees. This niftily runs through a series of small parks with monuments to reach the River Tyne Marina. Turn left and follow the periphery of the marina, turning right to cross a bridge. The cycle path leaves the marina to emerge onto a quiet road. Climb for a short distance then take the first right turn where views of Tynemouth are unfurled. ▶

A direct route through Smith's Dock has now reopened. Follow the road, which swings downhill to a roundabout near the slightly hidden Tyne Foot Passenger Ferry Terminal. The terminal, only 80m or so after the roundabout, is easily missed: it is down an innocuous looking side street opposite the ornate brown-tiled Crane House – a former pub.

If you have missed the last ferry, which is particularly easily done on a Sunday, adopt either the Alternative Tynemouth ending or if you're determined to reach South Shields, retrace the route to connect with the Running late alternative ending (see end of Day 3 route description).

The imposing statue of Admiral Collingwood, second in command at the Battle of Trafalgar, can be seen in the distance at Tynemouth.

FERRY TIMES

At the time of writing the ferry costs £1.70 one way or £2.90 return (bicycles carried free of charge), with the crossings to South Shields at the following times:

- **Sunday 10.15am every 30min until 5.45pm**
- Monday–Wednesday 6.45am every 30min until 7.45pm
- Thursday–Saturday 6.45am every 30min until 10.40pm

The ferry trends SSE across a scenic stretch of the river and takes you, as the crow flies, a little farther from the end of the route. Having disembarked on the south side of the Tyne, take a left immediately off the gang-plank, initially beside the river (**the Running Late alternative ending re-joins here**). This leads through a quiet docklands development and along Wapping Street.

At the T-junction take care turning right uphill onto the sometimes busy River Drive. A left off this after 150m leads onto Greens Place. After 200m, turn right onto Baring Street where the unmistakable **Arbeia Roman Fort** with its replica Roman buildings will be seen. There is a sign to commemorate the end of the route.

The **fort of Arbeia**, which marks the official end of the ride, once guarded the sea route to Hadrian's Wall and housed around 600 troops. As well as some existing remains, the barracks, gatehouse and officer's house have been rebuilt on their original foundations and the museum pays testament to the cosmopolitan nature of the troops stationed on and around the Wall area who journeyed from the far corners of the Roman Empire. The site is free to enter but can be difficult to catch for late finishing cyclists. It is open April–September, 10am–5pm on weekdays, and until 4pm on weekends.

No coast-to-coast route is truly over until the sea-front has been reached. From the finishing sign, head back down to Green Place, turn right and follow it to a roundabout. Go downhill in the direction of the cannon to follow a shared use path through a park. Turn left on the broad River Drive, followed by a right into the first car park and a series of sculptures 'The Conversation Piece'.

Success! The finish at Arbeia Roman Fort

'The Conversation Piece', South Shields

South Shields' surprisingly golden harbour beach lies beyond, offering expansive views of the historic Spanish Battery (Tynemouth Headland) with its Castle, Priory and imposing Admiral Collingwood monument. There is a set of free public toilets only 200m or so south of 'The Conversation Piece' and a limited selection of places to get food including a fish and chip shop 400m further along the coast by the Ocean Beach Pleasure Park.

Running late alternative to South Shields
(using Tyne Pedestrian and Cycle Tunnel)

It is not unheard of to get caught out by the last ferry crossing to South Shields, especially on a Sunday. If you're running too late for the ferry, then using the Tyne cycle tunnel and National Cycle Route 14 is an option. Although this route is on shared use cycle paths or on traffic calmed roads, many of the cycle paths are beside noisy roads without views of the Tyne. The riding on this side of the river from Jarrow to South Shields is not in any way pleasant and should not be considered if the ferry crossing is an option. The surreal cycle tunnel is good, however.

After Armstrong Road and Auburn Close there is a T-junction where HCW goes left. Head diagonally rightwards here onto the dead end Norman Terrace. After

Looking north to the Spanish Battery from South Shields beach

200m turn right up the bollarded Cumberland Street. At the T-junction bear diagonally left to cross the A187 and use a cycle path, turning right down Coach Open to reach the **Tyne Pedestrian and Cycle Tunnel**. Cyclists should use the lift. Once underground, the tunnel for cyclists is on the right. Follow cycling signs to South Shields and National Cycle Route 14 – the Keelmans Way. A cycle path leads away from the river on top of the course of the road tunnel and beside its peculiar giant air vent funnel. The path eventually reaches a T-junction with the A185. Turn left and suffer a shared use cycle path beside the busy A185 and then A194 for a couple of miles towards South Shields. Having passed by the Port of Tyne, you'll reach a roundabout where you need to make a left turn by a metal sculpture of a centurion, a cyclist and the comedian Sarah Millican to an immediate right at the next mini roundabout.

Head uphill and along St Eldon Street to its conclusion, where a path in the same line leads to Laygate. A left on this is followed by an immediate right onto a cycle path. The path is narrow and emerges at a roundabout negotiated by a shared use path. Take a left turn on an easily missed cycle path in 50m to sneak behind a Wickes store. At the end of the cycle path turn right. At the large roundabout bear left down to the Shields Ferry Terminal where you can now follow the normal ending to HCW.

Alternative Tynemouth ending

An alternative ending in **Tynemouth** on the promontory of the Spanish Battery is a reasonably satisfying conclusion (it is the ending of the C2C and Reivers Route and a sign formerly marked it as a potential start of HCW based on the idea that HCW can function as an E–W return route for the C2C). Continue on National Cycle Route 1 along the riverfront for ¼ mile or so then take a right turn at the Staith House pub to reach the promenade. This shared use path is delightful; there is a sting in its tail as a ramp heads steeply leftwards uphill – usually interrupted by a mandatory photo at the finishing sign. There is a car park (fee) at the top with several easily reached small beaches beyond it. Celebratory sustenance can be purchased by following Pier Road for 400m to reach the popular Front Street, with its wide selection of restaurants, pubs, cafés and takeaways.

Comedian Sarah Millican, a cyclist and a centurion

BICYCLES ON THE METRO

Outside of rush hour, bicycles are now tolerated on the Metro rail network on certain routes. Ensure lifts are used. Taking bicycles on the Metro appears to be partly at the guards' discretion. We personally have taken bicycles on one weekday post-7pm Metro train from South Shields to Newcastle Central Station with no trouble.

To South Shields Metro Station: from Arbeia Roman Fort, continue uphill along Baring Street, and then down the hill to meet a crossroads. Turn right along Ocean Road then dismount for the pedestrianised high street where the Metro station is found at the unmissable rail bridge.

It is worth checking with the guard at South Shields Metro Station for the most up-to-date information as cyclists heading to Newcastle Central Station may be obliged to disembark at Gateshead Stadium Station and cycle the final short distance across the river: St James Road north, left on A184 cycle path for 300m, right down Albany Road signed 'Gateshead Quays', left on Quayside Road, straight on to Mill Road, left past the Baltic Centre to Millennium Bridge – follow signs to Newcastle Central Station thereafter.

EAST TO WEST

South Shields to Haltwhistle begins steadily enough as the Tyne is followed gradually upstream. In Corbridge, the one-way system means the route goes along Middle Street past the church with a right turn at the market square. E–W riders benefit from a helpful left turn after crossing Hexham Bridge that involves circulating through a tunnel to avoid a busy roundabout. The first significant climb is on a minor road leading towards Chesters Roman Fort, which is soon after followed by a long gradual ascent over Whinny Hill to Fourstones. These climbs announce the imminence of the Pennines. From Newbrough the high point of the route is reached by means of a climb that is never particularly steep but is protracted over the course of several miles; its duration easily makes it the toughest climb of the E–W crossing. There is the brief respite of a steepish descent before reaching a punchy climb from the dip at Vindolanda, which soon eases.

The truest finish – South Shields beach

OTHER ITINERARIES
The Wall Only – a shortened two-day version

Start	Bowness-on-Solway (NY 223 627)
Finish	South Shields (NZ 364 680)
Distance	100 miles (161km)
Total ascent	1660m
Steepest climb	Greenwhelt Bank nears 1 in 4
Time	2 days
Terrain	Predominantly on minor roads and surfaced cycle paths
OS maps	314, 315, OL43, 316
Refreshments	Refer to Day 2 and Day 3 of the standard Hadrian's Cycleway (HCW) route description
Intermediate distances	Carlisle, 14 miles; Brampton, 29 miles; Gilsland, 38 miles; Haltwhistle, 43 miles; Vindolanda, 51 miles; Newbrough, 58 miles; Hexham, 65 miles; Corbridge, 69 miles; Prudhoe, 76 miles; Tyne Bridge quayside, 88 miles; Wallsend, 93 miles; South Shields, 100 miles

While Coast-to-Coast versions of other northern Sustrans' routes are a big ask for average cyclists in two days, this excellent two-day version of HCW is well-suited to average time-pushed weekend warriors aiming to connect two coastlines, yet wanting to capture the essence of the Roman-themed ride. It is also particularly suited to incorporating the tremendous More Wall Alternative – which we recommend. By starting at Bowness-on-Solway, Day 1 of the three-day HCW is not ridden and an advance start is made on Day 2 (Bowness to Haltwhistle is 43 miles). The Wall Only route makes a good one-day challenge for seasoned super-fit cyclists.

GETTING TO BOWNESS-ON-SOLWAY

Unfortunately Bowness-on-Solway is not on the rail network so a further truncation can be made by beginning the ride in Carlisle 14 miles further east, but this takes away the full Wall and coast-to-coast elements.

Guided group admiring the Wall at Steel Rigg with Peel Crags and Craig Lough beyond (Day 1, MWA)

Bowness-on-Solway can be reached with 10 extra miles from the railway station in Wigton (giving an entirely viable 53-mile first day to Haltwhistle).

To connect from Wigton Station, cross the pedestrian bridge over the A595, turn right, and go north through housing estate cul-de-sacs on Standingstone Heights. Turn right on Cross Lane. Turn left at T-junction. Follow signs to Oulton, then Kirkbride where there is a left on a hill to Anthorn. At the T-junction before Anthorn turn right, then left, following signs to Bowness-on-Solway.

Day 1: Bowness-on-Solway to Haltwhistle
Your day begins at the 'distance to Rome' signpost at the west end of Bowness-on-Solway. From there, follow the Day 2 route description as per the official HCW or adopt the More Wall Alternative (MWA) by following the route description in Day 2A.

Day 2: Haltwhistle to South Shields
For those who followed the route of the official HCW yesterday, Day 2 will start in Haltwhistle. If you followed the MWA on Day 1, you'll start the day in Once Brewed. Follow the standard Day 3 version of the route to reach South Shields.

APPENDIX A
Accommodation

Location	Type	Name	Phone	Website or email	Evening meal available	En route	Bike storage
						Nearby = a distance of less than 1km	
Ravenglass	Camping	Camping and Caravan club	01229 717250	ravenglass.campsite@ thefriendlyclub.co.uk		Yes	
Ravenglass	B&B	Bay Horse	01524 424 000	www.bayhorseravenglass.co.uk		Yes	
Ravenglass	Hotel	The Inn	01229 717230	www.theinnatravenglass.co.uk	Yes	Yes	
Ravenglass	Guest house	Rosegarth	01229 717275	www.rose-garth.co.uk		Yes	
Holmrook	Camping, pods, cottages	Shepherds Views	01946 729907	www.shepherdsviewsholidays. co.uk		Yes	
Seascale	B&B	Westcliff	01946 728298	www.westcliffhotel.net		Yes	
Seascale	Hotel	Calder House	01946 728538	www.calderhouse.co.uk	Yes	Yes	Yes
Egremont	Bunk barn	Horse and Groom	01946 758198			Yes	
Whitehaven	Hotel	Chase	01946 693656	www.chasewhitehaven.co.uk	Yes	Yes	Yes
Whitehaven	Guest House	Glenard	01946 692249			Yes	
Workington	Hotel	Morven House	01900 602118	www.morvenguesthouse.com	Yes	Yes	Yes
Workington	B&B	Dower House	01900 605906	www.dowerhouse-workington. co.uk		Nearby	Yes

Location	Type	Name	Phone	Website or email	Evening meal available	En route	Bike storage
Maryport	B&B	Riverside	01900 813595				
Allonby	Hotel	Ship	01900 881017	www.theshipallonby.co.uk	Yes	Yes	Yes
Allonby	B&B	Brookside	01900 881576			Yes	Yes
Silloth	B&B	Queens	01524 251580	www.bedandbreakfast-silloth.co.uk		Yes	Yes
Silloth	Camping, caravans	Moordale	01697 331375	www.springlea.co.uk/moordale		1km off route	
Silloth	B&B	Greenview	07763 881737			Yes	
Silloth	Hotel	Golf Hotel	01697 331438	www.golfhotelsilloth.co.uk		Yes	
Silloth	B&B	Old Chapel	01697 351126		Pub nearby	Yes	Yes
Bowness-on-Solway	Guest house, wigwams, camping	Wallsend	01697 351055	www.wallsend.net	Pub nearby	Yes	Yes
Bowness-on-Solway	Pub	Kings Arms	01697 351426	www.kingsarmsbowness.co.uk	Yes	Yes	
Bowness-on-Solway	Camping, bunk barn	Kirkland House	01697 351400		Pub nearby	Yes	
Port Carlisle	Lodges, wigwams, camping	Roman Wall Lodges	07784 736423	www.hadrians-wall-accommodation.co.uk	Pub nearby	Yes	

123

Location	Type	Name	Phone	Website or email	Evening meal available	En route	Bike storage
Carlisle	Hotel	Crown and Mitre	01228 525491	www.rownandmitre-hotel-carlisle.com	Yes	Yes	
Carlisle	Guest house	Hazel Dean	01228 711953	www.hazeldeantherapycentre.com	Yes	Yes	Yes
Carlisle	B&B	Tantallin	01228 550209			2km off route	
Carlisle	Hostel	City Hostel	07914 720821	www.carlislecityhostel.com		Nearby	Yes
Crosby on Eden	Bunk barn	Bluebell	01228 573600		Pub nearby	Nearby	Yes
Brampton	Bunkhouse	Florries on the Wall	01697 741704	www.florriesonthewall.co.uk	Yes	Nearby	
Brampton	Pub	Howard Arms	01697 742758	www.howardarmsbrampton.co.uk	Yes	Yes	
Lanercost	B&B	Lanercost	01697 742589				
Greenhead	Hotel, bunkhouse	Greenhead	01697 747411	www.greenheadhotel.com	Yes	Yes	Yes
Greenhead	Camping barn	Holmhead	01697 747402		Pub nearby	Yes	
Gilsland	B&B	Brookside Villa	01697 747300	www.brooksidevilla.com	Yes	Yes	Yes
Gilsland	B&B	Hollies on the Wall	01697 747267	www.theholliesonthewall.co.uk	Pub nearby	Yes	
Haltwhistle	Guest house	Ashcroft	01434 320213	www.ashcroftguesthouse.co.uk	Pub nearby	Yes	

Location	Type	Name	Phone	Website or email	Evening meal available	En route	Bike storage
Haltwhistle	Hotel	Centre of Britain	01434 322422	www.centreofbritain.co.uk	Yes	Yes	
Haltwhistle	B&B	Old School House	01434 312013	www.oldschoolhousehaltwhistle.com	Pub nearby	Yes	Yes
Haltwhistle	B&B	Belford House	01434 322572	www.belfordhouserooms.co.uk	Pub nearby	Yes	
Haltwhistle	Camping, pods, lodges	Herding Hill Farm	01434 320175	www.herdinghillfarm.co.uk	Yes	2km off route	
Melkridge	Camping, bunk barn	Hadrians Wall Campsite	01434 320495	www.hadrianswallcampsite.co.uk		Nearby	
Bardon Mill	Hotel	Bowes	01434 344237		Yes	Yes	
Once Brewed	YHA hostel	The Sill	0800 0191 700	www.yha.org.uk	Yes	MWA/1km off route	Yes
Once Brewed	Pub/inn	Twice Brewed	01434 344534	www.twicebrewedinn.co.uk	Yes	MWA/1km off route	
Once Brewed	Camping	Winshields Farm	07968 102780	www.winshieldscampsite.co.uk		MWA/1km off route	
Haydon Bridge	B&B	Reading Rooms	01434 688802	www.thereadingrooms haydonbridge.co.uk		3km off route	
Hindshield	B&B, groups	Hadrian Lodge	01434 684867		Yes	Yes	
Newbrough	Bunkhouse	Newbrough	07707 778094	www.newbroughbunkhouse.co.uk		Yes	Yes
Newbrough	Pub	Red Lion	01434 674226	www.redlionnewbrough.co.uk	Yes	Yes	

Location	Type	Name	Phone	Website or email	Evening meal available	En route	Bike storage
Newbrough	B&B	Westfield	01434 674241	www.westfieldbandb.co.uk			
Hexham	B&B	Hexham Town B&B	07714 292602	www.hexhamtownbedandbreakfast.co.uk	Yes	Yes	
Hexham	B&B	Burncrest	01434 601444			Nearby	
Hexham/ Warden	Inn	Boatside	01434 602233		Yes	Yes	
Corbridge	Pub	Golden Lion	01434 632216	www.goldenlioncorbridge.co.uk	Yes	Yes	Yes
Corbridge	B&B	Fellcroft	01434 632384		Nearby	Yes	Yes
Prudhoe	B&B	Ovington House	01661 832442		Nearby	Nearby	Yes
Ovingham	Camping, pods	High Hermitage	07974 461053	www.highhermitagecaravanpark.co.uk		1km off route	
Wylam	Pub	Boathouse	01661 853431		Yes	Yes	
Wylam	Pub	Black Bull	01661 853112	www.blackbullwylam.co.uk	Yes	Yes	
Wylam	Camping	Stephensons Arms	07967 320405		Nearby	Yes	
Newcastle	YHA hostel	Newcastle Central YHA	0345 260 2583	www.yha.org.uk	Nearby	Nearby	Yes
South Shields	B&B	Annie's	0191 456 6088	www.anniesguesthouse.co.uk		Nearby	
South Shields	Hotel	Littlehaven	0191 455 4455	www.littlehavenhotel.com	Yes	Yes	

APPENDIX B

Bike shops and other useful contacts

Bike shops in route order

Cleator Moor
Ainfield Cycles
Jacktrees Road
CA23 3DW
tel 01946 812427
www.ainfieldcycles.co.uk

Whitehaven
Haven Cycles
2 Preston Street
LA1 1NZ
tel 01946 63236
www.havencycles-c2cservices.co.uk

Workington
Halfords
Derwent Drive Retail Park
CA14 3YW
tel 01900 601635
www.halfords.com

Carlisle
Scotby Cycles
Church Street
CA2 5TL
tel 01228 546931
www.scotbycycles.co.uk

Palace Cycles
120–124 Botchergate
CA1 1SH
tel 01228 523142
www.palacecycles.co.uk

Bikeseven
1 Market Street
CA3 8QJ
tel 01228 739926
www.bikeseven.co.uk

Prudhoe
Giant
Princess Court
NE42 6PL
tel 01661 830618
www.giant-newcastle.co.uk

Cycle Art
Princess Court
NE42 6PL
tel 01661 835603
www.cycle-art.co.uk

Gateshead
Backyard Bike Shop
Hillgate Quay
NE8 2BH
www.backyardbikeshop.com

Newcastle
The Cycle Hub
Quayside
NE6 1BU
tel 0191 276 7250
www.thecyclehub.org

Edinburgh Bicycle
5–7 Union Road
Byker
NE6 1EH
tel 0191 265 8619

Cycle Surgery
60–62 Northumberland Street
NE1 7DF
tel 0191 221 2709
www.cyclesurgery.com

South Shields

Conway Cycles
12 Salem Street
NE33 1HH
tel 0191 455 3579

AS Cycles
44A St Aiden's Road
NE33 2HD
tel 0191 456 3133
www.ascycles.co.uk

Cycle/baggage transport

Pedal Power
tel 01665 713448 or 07790 596782
www.pedal-power.co.uk

Baggage Transfer Plus
tel 07545 086857
www.baggagetransferplus.com

The Bicycle Transport Co
tel 01297 240400
www.thebicycletransportcompany.co.uk

Eco Cycle Adventures
tel 01434 610076
www.ecocycleadventures.co.uk

The Bike Bus Stanley Travel
tel 01207 237424
www.stanley-travel.com/the-bike-bus

Companies that arrange accommodation and transport as a package

Trailbrakes
tel 01416 286676 or 07922 653327
www.trailbrakes.co.uk

CycleActive
tel 01768 840400
www.cycleactive.com

Peak tours
tel 01457 851462
www.peak-tours.com

Skedaddle
tel 0191 2651110
www.skedaddle.com

APPENDIX C
Further reading

There are literally hundreds of books about Hadrian's Wall, below is a small sample.

Mark Richards, *Hadrian's Wall Path* (Cicerone, 2015) – the best walking guide to the Wall, and worth bringing along on the bike if you're intending to add some extended walks to your tour.

Simon Forty, *Hadrian's Wall Operations Manual: From Construction to World Heritage Site* (Sparkford: Haynes, 2018) – In the tradition of the classic Haynes mechanic's manuals, this is a superb take on the Wall and its history, with every factoid you need to know; it is an excellent place to start.

Rory Stewart, *The Marches: Border Walks with my Father* (London: Penguin, 2016) – a personal story about the borderlands, much of which is centred on Hadrian's Wall and its legacy in the form of distinct divisions around the Anglo-Scots border. The book benefits greatly from the author's on-the-ground experiences, philosophical musings and eye for detail. The comparison between the Roman's construction of the Wall and US-Anglo operations in Afghanistan is particularly illuminating. The book offers an intriguing insight into the significance of the Wall to British culture and identities, but also detailed experiences of other locations visited by Hadrian's Cycleway – such as the Cardurnock Peninsula.

Adrian Goldsworthy, *Hadrian's Wall* (London: Head of Zeus, 2018) – a clear, concise and interesting history book.

Nick Hodgson, *Hadrian's Wall* (London: Hale, 2017) – a book with greater archaeological emphasis than many Wall histories.

Brian Dobson and David J Breeze, *Hadrian's Wall* (London: Penguin, 2000) – first published in the 1970s, this is a well-known account of the Wall.

Alan Michael Whitworth, *Hadrian's Wall through Time* (Stroud: Amberly, 2012) – a fascinating and distinctive take on Wall history that makes comparisons between how the Wall was and what is found today.

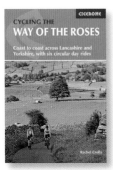
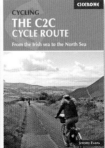
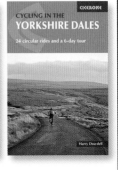
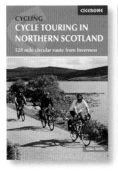
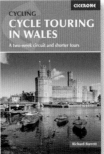

Passing Milecastle 42 on the More Wall Alternative (Day 2A)

DOWNLOAD THE ROUTES
IN GPX FORMAT

All the routes in this guide are available for download from:

www.cicerone.co.uk/1042/GPX

as GPX files. You should be able to load them into most formats of mobile device, whether GPS or smartphone.

When you go to this link, you will be asked for your email address and where you purchased the guide, and have the option to subscribe to the Cicerone e-newsletter.

LISTING OF CICERONE GUIDES

SCOTLAND

Backpacker's Britain:
   Northern Scotland
Ben Nevis and Glen Coe
Cycle Touring in Northern Scotland
Cycling in the Hebrides
Great Mountain Days in Scotland
Mountain Biking in Southern and
   Central Scotland
Mountain Biking in West and North
   West Scotland
Not the West Highland Way
Scotland
Scotland's Best Small Mountains
Scotland's Mountain Ridges
The Ayrshire and Arran Coastal Paths
The Border Country
The Borders Abbeys Way
The Cape Wrath Trail
The Great Glen Way
The Great Glen Way Map Booklet
The Hebridean Way
The Hebrides
The Isle of Mull
The Isle of Skye
The Skye Trail
The Southern Upland Way
The Speyside Way
The Speyside Way Map Booklet
The West Highland Way
Walking Highland Perthshire
Walking in Scotland's Far North
Walking in the Angus Glens
Walking in the Cairngorms
Walking in the Ochils, Campsie Fells
   and Lomond Hills
Walking in the Pentland Hills
Walking in the Southern Uplands
Walking in Torridon
Walking Loch Lomond and
   the Trossachs
Walking on Arran
Walking on Harris and Lewis
Walking on Jura, Islay and Colonsay
Walking on Rum and the Small Isles
Walking on the Orkney and
   Shetland Isles
Walking on Uist and Barra
Walking the Corbetts
   Vol 1 South of the Great Glen
Walking the Corbetts
   Vol 2 North of the Great Glen
Walking the Galloway Hills
Walking the Munros Vol 1 – Southern,
   Central and Western Highlands
Walking the Munros Vol 2 – Northern
   Highlands and the Cairngorms
West Highland Way Map Booklet
Winter Climbs Ben Nevis and
   Glen Coe
Winter Climbs in the Cairngorms

NORTHERN ENGLAND TRAILS

Hadrian's Wall Path
Hadrian's Wall Path Map Booklet
Pennine Way Map Booklet
The Coast to Coast Map Booklet
The Coast to Coast Walk
The Dales Way
The Dales Way Map Booklet
The Pennine Way

LAKE DISTRICT

Cycling in the Lake District
Great Mountain Days in the
   Lake District
Lake District Winter Climbs
Lake District:
   High Level and Fell Walks
Lake District:
   Low Level and Lake Walks
Mountain Biking in the Lake District
Outdoor Adventures with Children –
   Lake District
Scrambles in the Lake District – North
Scrambles in the Lake District – South
Short Walks in Lakeland Book 2:
   North Lakeland
The Cumbria Way
The Southern Fells
Tour of the Lake District
Trail and Fell Running in the Lake
   District
Walking the Lake District Fells –
   Langdale
Walking the Lake District Fells –
   Wasdale

NORTH WEST ENGLAND AND THE ISLE OF MAN

Cycling the Pennine Bridleway
Cycling the Way of the Roses
Isle of Man Coastal Path
The Lancashire Cycleway
The Lune Valley and Howgills
The Ribble Way
Walking in Cumbria's Eden Valley
Walking in Lancashire
Walking in the Forest of Bowland
   and Pendle
Walking on the Isle of Man
Walking on the West Pennine Moors
Walks in Ribble Country
Walks in Silverdale and Arnside

NORTH EAST ENGLAND, YORKSHIRE DALES AND PENNINES

Cycling in the Yorkshire Dales
Great Mountain Days in the Pennines
Mountain Biking in the
   Yorkshire Dales
South Pennine Walks

St Oswald's Way and St Cuthbert's
   Way
The Cleveland Way and the Yorkshire
   Wolds Way
The Cleveland Way Map Booklet
The North York Moors
The Reivers Way
The Teesdale Way
Trail and Fell Running in the
   Yorkshire Dales
Walking in County Durham
Walking in Northumberland
Walking in the North Pennines
Walking in the Yorkshire Dales:
   North and East
Walking in the Yorkshire Dales:
   South and West
Walks in the Yorkshire Dales

WALES AND WELSH BORDERS

Cycle Touring in Wales
Cycling Lon Las Cymru
Glyndwr's Way
Great Mountain Days in Snowdonia
Hillwalking in Shropshire
Hillwalking in Wales – Vol 1
Hillwalking in Wales – Vol 2
Mountain Walking in Snowdonia
Offa's Dyke Map Booklet
Offa's Dyke Path
Pembrokeshire Coast Path
   Map Booklet
Ridges of Snowdonia
Scrambles in Snowdonia
Snowdonia: Low-level and easy
   walks – North
The Cambrian Way
The Ceredigion and Snowdonia
   Coast Paths
The Pembrokeshire Coast Path
The Severn Way
The Snowdonia Way
The Wales Coast Path
The Wye Valley Walk
Walking in Carmarthenshire
Walking in Pembrokeshire
Walking in the Forest of Dean
Walking in the Wye Valley
Walking on the Brecon Beacons
Walking on the Gower
Walking the Shropshire Way

DERBYSHIRE, PEAK DISTRICT AND MIDLANDS

Cycling in the Peak District
Dark Peak Walks
Scrambles in the Dark Peak
Walking in Derbyshire
White Peak Walks:
   The Northern Dales
White Peak Walks:
   The Southern Dales

For full information on all our guides,
books and eBooks, visit our website:
www.cicerone.co.uk

Explore the world with Cicerone

walking • trekking • mountaineering • climbing • mountain biking • cycling • via ferratas • scrambling • trail running • skills and techniques

For over 50 years, Cicerone have built up an outstanding collection of nearly 400 guides, inspiring all sorts of amazing experiences.

www.cicerone.co.uk – where adventures begin

- Our **website** is a treasure-trove for every outdoor adventurer. You can buy books or read inspiring articles and trip reports, get technical advice, check for updates, and view videos, photographs and mapping for routes and treks.

- **Register this book** or any other Cicerone guide in your member's library on our website and you can choose to automatically access updates and GPX files for your books, if available.

- Our **fortnightly newsletters** will update you on new publications and articles and keep you informed of other news and events. You can also follow us on Facebook, Twitter and Instagram.

We hope you have enjoyed using this guidebook. If you have any comments you would like to share, please contact us using the form on our website or via email, so that we can provide the best experience for future customers.

CICERONE

Juniper House, Murley Moss Business Village, Oxenholme Road, Kendal LA9 7RL

✉ info@cicerone.co.uk   cicerone.co.uk 🅕🅣🅘